KATHARINE HEPBURN

A STYLISH LIFE

JOAL RYAN

A BYRON PREISS BOOK

ST. MARTIN'S PRESS
NEW YORK

For M.M.

ACKNOWLEDGMENTS

Thanks to: Dinah Dunn, Byron Preiss, Clarice Levin, Tim Steger, and
J. Vita at Byron Preiss Visual Publications; Peter Rubie at Perkins,
Rubie Associates; Elizabeth Beier and Rebecca Schuman at
St. Martin's Press; and Gilda Hannah for her wonderful design.

ART CREDITS

Pages 2, 8, 9, 10, 11, 12, 15, 19, 24, 25, 28, 31, 32, 33, 35, 38, 40, 44-55, 60, 61,
62, 65, 70, 74, 75, 77-80, 82-91, 95, 98, 99, 101, 103, 104, 106, 108, 110, 112,
116, 118, 121-133, 141, 144-152, 154, 156-160, 162, 164, 167, 171-183, 186,
190, 192-198, 200, 203 © ARCHIVE PHOTOS; page 25 © ARCHIVE FRANCE/ARCHIVE
PHOTOS; page 143 © COLUMBIA PICTURES /ARCHIVE PHOTOS; pages 7, 76 ©
CORBIS/BETTMANN; page 97 © GENE LESTER/ARCHIVE PHOTOS; pages 8, 14, 19-20,
22-23, 41, 44, 56, 59, 66-67, 69, 71, 85, 92, 96, 105, 107, 115, 120, 134-135,
140, 153, 155, 161, 166, 169, 185, 189, 199, 204 ©GLOBE PHOTOS; pages 73, 81
© MGM/ARCHIVE PHOTOS; pages 27, 57 © MUSEUM OF THE CITY OF NEW YORK;
pages 17, 34 © POPPERFOTO/ ARCHIVE PHOTOS; pages 36, 39, 43 © RKO/ARCHIVE
PHOTOS; page 202 ©SONIA MOSKOWITZ/ARCHIVE PHOTOS; pages 137, 138 © UNITED
ARTISTS/ARCHIVE PHOTOS.

A Byron Preiss Book
Design by Gilda Hannah
Editor: Dinah Dunn

ISBN 0-312-24649-8

First Edition: September 1999

10 9 8 7 6 5 4 3 2 1

Books are available in quantity for promotional and premium use.
Write Director of Special Sales, St. Martin's Press, 175 Fifth Avenue,
New York, N.Y. 10010, for information on discounts and terms, or call
toll-free (800) 221-7945. In New York, call (212) 674-5151
(ext.645).

$\mathscr{K}$atharine Hepburn was born at the outset of the twentieth century. By the close, she was its most celebrated screen actress—period.

Hepburn won more Oscars, earned more nominations, spanned more years, and starred opposite more legendary leading men than anyone else. Only Marilyn Monroe trumped her as a world-class icon—no small feat, considering the convention-defying Hepburn wasn't exactly a washout in that category, either.

The notion that Hepburn was the most outstanding female presence of American film's last one hundred years is easily argued, if not proved. (See, for example, *The African Queen*, *The Philadelphia Story*, or *Woman of the Year*.) But the reasons why are harder to sketch out.

Hepburn was not as screen-pretty as a Grace Kelly. She was not as prolific as a Bette Davis. She was not as endearing as an Audrey Hepburn. She was not as universally praised by movie critics as a Meryl Streep. She was not as sultry as a Lauren Bacall or an Ava Gardner. She was not as personally compelling, in a soap-opera sort of way, as an Elizabeth Taylor.

She wasn't even "one of us." In a nation ostensibly so proud of its average American, Hepburn wasn't in the least bit statistically average. She was born well-off. After a brief marriage, she stayed single. And she never had children. She was more left than center. She was resolutely more upper-class than middle-class.

And yet . . . When Americans were asked, in a 1999 Zogby/Reuter poll, to select the "greatest" film actress of the century, Hepburn was the name that came to their lips first. She finished up there with the cowboy John Wayne—a man whose name is the very definition of movie star.

So again the question: Why?

Maybe it's the pants.

Katharine Hepburn was a walking, talking Gap ad before there was such a thing. She donned khakis (and trousers and slacks and . . .), to the eternal annoyance of Hollywood publicity executives and fashion mavens everywhere. She just didn't seem to care. Scratch that—she *didn't* care. She was brought up to work hard and believe in what she believed in, not to smile prettily and curtsy for the sake of a silly press conference. The spiritual parent of antistars such as Marlon Brando and Sean Penn, Hepburn didn't see the selling of the movie as important as the making of the movie. The thing with her was the job—the acting. She enjoyed the residual fame and wealth, but, perhaps owing to her manor-born status, she considered the celebrity's life a bothersome, boring chore. As a young star, she didn't want to talk to reporters. She didn't want to do the party scene. She didn't want Hollywood to think she wanted Hollywood. Hence the pants.

In our mind's eye, the pants let Hepburn be Hepburn—strong, assertive, comfortable. They put her on equal footing with men. They made her an early role model for the strong working woman. Hepburn, we think, can bring home the bacon, fry it up in the pan (the disastrous kitchen sequence of *Woman of the Year*, notwithstanding), and snag a man without so much as showing a little leg. Sure, maybe Bette Davis or Joan Crawford can do that, too, but surely not as well. They always seem more desperate, obvious, and unlucky—terribly unlucky, particularly in love. But not Hepburn. As singular a screen persona as she projected, she always got the guy—Cary Grant, Jimmy Stewart, Humphrey Bogart, Spencer Tracy, Henry Fonda. She was the smart girl who had it all—including the rail-thin figure. In truth, of course, Hepburn didn't seek, nor get it all. While Hepburn disciples broke their backs managing career, spouses, and children, Hepburn herself managed only Hepburn.

Still, the pants held so much promise. Perhaps, if we found the right pair—just like Hepburn . . .

Maybe it's the voice.

If not classically beautiful, Hepburn was utterly distinctive—the cheekbones, the fair, freckled skin, the hair (first worn wavy and long, then worn wavy and in a bun), the legs. And then there was the voice.

In the 1930s, a movie actress sounded like a movie actress sounded like a movie actress. In short, the American-born talent sounded like Ruby Keeler, á la *42nd Street*—a touch breathy, a touch stagy, a touch prone to enunciating every "eye" vowel sound with a soft "ah."

Enter Hepburn. She was no Ruby Keeler. Her vowels were pronounced the way they were supposed to be pronounced—particularly if you grew up in Connecticut and attended Bryn Mawr. Her syllables were sharp. Her cadence was clipped. The sound cut through so much clutter like a precision buzz saw. Hepburn's voice stood alone. Sometimes it annoyed, sometimes it fluttered away, and sometimes it threatened to pierce ears. But it stood alone.

You learn to hear a Hepburn movie before you learn to watch one. You recognize her as the lady with the Funny Voice. Then one day, you stop—and you listen. And suddenly you know what all the fuss is about.

Maybe it's the love story.

Tracy and Hepburn is as entertaining a modern-day romance as we have. It's got intrigue (he's married—not to her). It's got spark (he's stout and gruff; she's lithe and classy). It's got a semi-happy ending (yes, he dies—but he dies as one-half of a still-coupled couple).

He, of course, was Spencer Tracy. His legacy owes almost more to their love affair than hers does. Alone, he's an act in declining favor—respected on paper as a man capable of inhabiting many roles (the Portuguese fisherman in *Captains Courageous*, the priest in *Boys Town*, the slow-burning parent in *Father of the Bride*), but passed up in the real-world video store for lacking the "it" factor that makes a Humphrey Bogart picture as much a commodity in 1999 as it was in 1939. "I can't come up with a single line to associate with that

great actor," screenwriter William Goldman once wrote of Tracy. And that's the thing of it—no "it."

Except when he was with Hepburn.

With her, he was—and is—something special. *Woman of the Year*, *Adam's Rib*, and *Pat and Mike* are all standard-bearers of the smart romantic comedy. If you want to see how it's done—or how they're not doing it today—you go back to the source.

Our love affair with Tracy-Hepburn movies, of course, has as much to do with what's in our minds as what's on the screen. *Pat and Mike*, for instance, isn't exactly the most swiftly plotted film of all time, but we remember it as sharper and livelier because we imagine that's how the two great lovers were in real life—and we hope that's the kind of relationship (challenging, tender, respectful) we'll find in our real lives.

Never mind that the ideal is unattainable, never mind that not even Hepburn could vouch for how truly devoted Tracy was to the pairing—just keep on looking at Hepburn to give us hope of a Tracy-Hepburn.

In the end, perhaps the best argument as to why we're fixated on Katharine Hepburn is the most elemental: We love *the idea* of Katharine Hepburn.

We love that she did what she wanted—and did it well and did it for an impossibly long time. We love that she traveled first-class, in work and in life. We love that she never went camp like Bette Davis (*What Ever Happened to Baby Jane?*) or tabloid like Joan Crawford (the "Mommie Dearest" taint) or TV commercial like Elizabeth Taylor (whatever new perfume she's hawking these days). We love that she always seemed ready for adventure. We love that she golfed and swam and probably didn't throw at all like a girl.

We love that she made *The African Queen*.

And *The Philadelphia Story*.

And *Woman of the Year*.

And *Stage Door*.

And *Bringing Up Baby*.

And *On Golden Pond*.

We love that, after all that, she's Kate.

*K*atharine Houghton Hepburn, age three. Already plotting a brilliant career, no doubt. She definitely always wanted to be famous. "I didn't care what it was in," she said. "Win the race." She got off to a solid start, the eldest daughter of Dr. Thomas Hepburn, a doctor who specialized in the unmentionable (urology), and Katharine Martha Houghton, a scion of the Corning Glass family who also specialized in the unmentionable (suffrage, birth control, etc.). "Kath" was born in Hartford, Connecticut, on May 12, 1907—"despite everything I may have said to the contrary," she later confessed. For more than fifty years, Kath passed off November 8, 1909, as her birthday. It was a useful fib. Made the prodigy seem all the more prodigious.

*B*rother Tom (*on the left in the photo to the right*, in 1910) was Hepburn's first leading man, the one and only big brother. The entire clan (Dr. and Mrs. Hepburn, their six children, including Dick, Bob, Marion, and Peg) was tight, but Tom and Kath especially so. Tom died in 1921. Kath found him hanged at a family friend's house. He was only fifteen. To the family's eye, the press made a mess out things— insinuating suicide and such. Kath's father insisted the death was an accident. Tom was just trying out a rope trick, he said. Despite the devastating loss, the Hepburns moved on. And they added a healthy mistrust of the media to their baggage.

*B*y 1929, Kath (*left*), aspiring famous person, had become Kate, aspiring actress. She didn't look like the usual starlet—tall (a touch over five-seven), lean, freckled, and red-haired, instead of petite, soft, buxom, and blonde. She didn't sound like the usual starlet—not with that brittle Bryn Mawr College–speak (class of 1928). Fact was, Kate *wasn't* the usual starlet. Her most distinguishing characteristic was her attitude—she *had* one. Raised to be a freethinker, Kate thought freely and, often, out loud. Her extremely healthy sense of self-esteem helped her blow through regional theater in Baltimore—and helped her get fired from her very first almost-Broadway job (1928's *The Big Pond.*) They'd get used to her. They'd have to. "If you don't stick your head up or kick someone," she said, ". . . you're afraid you won't get noticed."

$\mathcal{H}$epburn, sitting pretty in an early glamour shot (*above*), virtually dared Hollywood not to hire her. The year was 1932. Kate was starring on Broadway as an amazon in *The Warrior's Husband*. She attracted quite a bit of attention as a larger-than-life specimen of he-womanhood. ("They didn't like me until I got into a leg show," she said.) RKO—the studio of, appropriately, *King Kong*—came calling. (Paramount did, too. But she flunked the screen test there.) Producer David O. Selznick needed an actress to play opposite the legendary John Barrymore in a melodrama called *A Bill of Divorcement*. He offered Kate five hundred dollars a week. She wanted fifteen hundred. He offered seven hundred fifty. She wanted fifteen hundred. He offered one thousand. She *still* wanted fifteen hundred. Supposedly Kate named a price she didn't think RKO would meet. The joke was on Hollywood. Kate got her fifteen hundred.

*N*othing much impressed Kate. Not even John Barrymore (*at right*), of the "stars of stage and screen" Barrymores. The first day on the set of 1932's *A Bill of Divorcement*, Kate eyed her venerable costar doing prop work—"fiddling around with some pipes on the mantelpiece," she said. A Barrymore or no, Kate thought he was "overdoing it a bit." (Turned out, she was the one overdoing it, she later conceded.) For his part, Barrymore thought Hepburn a "creature *most* strange." They simply existed in different worlds. Barrymore, at fifty, was in slow decline. (His ill-worn liver would give out in 1942.) Hepburn, at twenty-five, was in swift ascent. Accordingly, on film, they played estranged father and daughter. Barrymore was Hillary Fairchild, a broken war veteran who returns home from a mental institution; Hepburn was Sydney, the good daughter who puts her own marriage on hold to care for him. First-class tearjerker material. First-rate reviews. Said the *New York Post*: "Miss Hepburn has the makings of a star."

$\mathcal{A}$ *Bill of Divorcement* was Kate's first film with George Cukor (*above*). Cukor, in Hollywood parlance, was a "woman's director." The best supporting evidence of this title (both compliment and vague put-down—one that later apparently cost him Clark Gable's favor as well as his job on *Gone with the Wind*) was the catty 1939 classic, *The Women*. In all, he worked with every diva from Joan Crawford to Norma Shearer, from Jean Harlow to Katharine Hepburn (*left*, with *Divorcement* costars Barrymore and Henry Stephenson). Ten times Kate and Cukor worked together—through eight films and two TV movies. The remarkable relationship began on a not-so-remarkable note. "I've just seen a test of the girl I want for *Bill of Divorcement*," Cukor told a journalist visiting the RKO lot in 1932. "She looks like a boa constrictor on a fast, but she's great!" She was also, as her director would learn, argumentative, opinionated, and obstinate. With Cukor, it was a fair fight. Kate respected that—respected him. Cukor was more than a "woman's director," Kate knew. He was an actor's director.

$\mathcal{C}$lear-eyed Kate (*opposite*) didn't come to Hollywood to knock around the B-movie bush leagues. She sought out the best—and got the best. *A Bill of Divorcement* not only launched her screen career but also set its tone: A-list talent behind the camera (Cukor); A-list talent in front of the camera, including Barrymore and Billie Burke (*above, at right*), best known as Glinda, the Good Witch of the North in *The Wizard of Oz*. A more mature Kate would say she was "lucky" for the opportunity. The twenty-something Kate didn't have the benefit of perspective. She simply saw herself as good—and deserving. By way of an excuse for her myopic tendencies, let it be noted that there was an eye injury that she suffered en route to Hollywood. Happened on a steamer train. She was making the trek west with friend, fellow actress, and future housemate Laura Harding. Their train was just outside Albuquerque. Kate, standing on a back platform, took a steel-filing fragment to the left eye. Scratched a cornea. Quite an unsightly thing. By the time Kate arrived at RKO, the studio's new, fifteen-hundred-dollars-a-week leading lady was sporting bloodshot action that even a notorious imbiber like Barrymore could admire. "Mr. Cukor!" she said, in typical understatement ". . . I have something in my eye!"

*K*ate wanted *Morning Glory* (1933). Saw the script in the office of producer Pandro S. Berman (*Top Hat, Father of the Bride*). Read it a little, and that was it—she *wanted* it. Never mind that Constance Bennett (*Topper*) was lined up as the star. It was all about Kate now. Berman acquiesced. He let her have *Morning Glory*, assigning actor/director Lowell Sherman (*She Done Him Wrong*) the task of corralling the resident comet. Kate saw magic screen-time potential in *Morning Glory*'s Eva Lovelace, the eager young actress trying to make a go of it on the cruel New York stage scene. The *New York Times* found Lovelace a "proud" and "captivating" woman who, at times, "has some weird notions"—all descriptions that to some degree would be applied to Kate herself. There was no getting around that Kate did have "weird notions"—especially for a contract player of the strong-arm studio era. "I was never a victim of the times I lived in," she said. And, professionally, she wasn't. The fame she so pursued was fame on her own terms. Kate wanted her pick of scripts, control of her career—and not a thing to do with the dreaded press and publicity people. RKO could have tired of her aloof Connecticut Yankee act. But it didn't (not yet anyway). A year into her film career, she was the studio's biggest actress except for Ginger Rogers. *Morning Glory*, costarring dashing leading-man type Douglas Fairbanks, Jr. (*left, opposite*), as one of Eva's suitors, opened at New York's Radio City Music Hall in August 1933 to acclaim. The *Times*, in an overall dismissive review of the material, singled out its star for "an ingratiating portrayal." Hepburn, the antistar star, had arrived. There'd be no dealing with her now (unless you were Cukor—and you yelled). Hollywood was in trouble. Kate had decided she was quite fond of movies—especially the camera. "The Morning Glory" was far from finished blooming.

istrionics of *Morning* ...
h Fairbanks (*at left*),
Hepburn her first
Award nomination.
March 16, 1934, she
irst Oscar. As was her
MO, Kate ducked the
nner, because she was
e country (both a con-
excuse and true). In
e Oscars weren't quite
ARS! (lights, cameras,
rs) of the multimedia
ceremony (a glorified
eally) was six years
ut the same age as
ed talkies. It was a
ping industry event,
age of which the *New*
es buried on page 10,
ne obituary of a Long
ewspaper editor. Not
would have showed if
ht it more prestigious.
ed outrageous fortune,
the best parts—but
le, gold men? To her,
itself was "the real
Besides, said the urol-
aughter, who never
one of her four Oscars
, the ceremony "would
yspepsia."

$\mathcal{S}$uccess—in all its foreign sports car glory. Not even Kate's patented stiff upper lip could remain unmoved by setting out to conquer the world (or a little corner of it) and winning. Broadway star, 1932. Movie star, 1932. Bigger movie star, 1933. Oscar winner, 1934. Joan Crawford? Bette Davis? Nobody made it that fast. Nobody else was the reigning "World's Best Movie Actress," as chosen by an international film exposition that year in Venice. No, she didn't really know what she was doing yet. Didn't really have command of the voice yet. But those were details. She was, after all, Katharine Hepburn. As her future *Woman of the Year* director George Stevens said, "I think she believed in those days that God had smitten her very young, and by a miracle made a Bernhardt."

The starlet—no, *star* it was now—had her pick of men. And she picked them. The agent/producer Leland Hayward, the aviator/mogul Howard Hughes—and the husband/insurance broker Ludlow Ogden Smith. Not many knew she was married, but she was. (And what people didn't know, they made up—whispering that Kate was a lesbian due to her house-sharing arrangement with Laura Harding.) Fact was, Kate married Smith, a beau she'd met at Bryn Mawr, on December 12, 1928, in Connecticut. Deciding it was best that her married name not tag her as Kate Smith (like the singer), the new bride persuaded "Luddy" to change *his* name—to S. Ogden Ludlow. After all the machinations were played out, Kate never used her married name. And she never much used the marriage.

*I*n between the splashy debut in *A Bill of Divorcement* and the star-making triumph of *Morning Glory*, came *Christopher Strong* (1933). It was a little film, most notable for the gender, if not the name, of its director. Dorothy Arzner was that rare Hollywood specimen—the woman director. Kate, being Kate, said she didn't think the situation was strange at all. That left the rest of the world to be amazed that in an age where an actress—oh, say Hepburn—could near-scandalize the public by wearing (gasp!) slacks, a woman could land a job shouting, "Action!" on a soundstage. If only *Christopher Strong* were as remarkable. The movie, starring Colin Clive in the title role, told the tale of a would-be love affair between a member of British Parliament (Clive) and a female pilot (Hepburn). Even outside the cockpit, Kate (*above*) was flying high and plotting her triumphant return to Broadway—otherwise known as her jump in *The Lake*.

$\mathcal{T}$his was how *The Lake* was supposed to proceed: A devastating Kate walks onstage; deeply moved critics and crowds lavish praise on the newly crowned queen of Hollywood. Except, for the first time in Kate's career, life did not imitate fairy tale—or a scene from *Morning Glory*. Instead of reliable Adolphe Menjou as a smitten producer, Hepburn had Jed Harris. Harris was the man who brought *The Front Page* and other hits to Broadway. In 1933, he launched *The Lake*, an imported English drama. Hepburn was the star— but one who felt out of her element and out of her league. Opening night was a disaster. Her voice, Kate said, "went all loony." (Being flat-out petrified can do that to one's vocal cords.) She worked through the show's run to improve the performance, but it was too late. Harris broke her, critics panned her, audiences ignored her. *The Lake* closed February 10, 1934, after fifty-five performances, and one infamous crack from critic Dorothy Parker: something about Hepburn running "the gamut of emotions from A to B."

*I*f Kate was lost in *The Lake*, she was utterly connected in *Little Women* (*opposite*). The 1933 film was the first sound version of the oft-adapted Louisa May Alcott novel—and, arguably, the definitive version. Not as prissy as the 1949 June Allyson Technicolor special. Not as pedantic as the 1994 Winona Ryder offering. Just clean and simple and as no-fuss as its black-and-white palette. For the time, the movie was considered the quintessential Hepburn performance in the quintessential Hepburn movie. For the public's money, Kate *was* Jo March. They shared the same background; indeed, they shared the same voice. Eastern-bred, spunky, unbowed, ambitious, in awe of their parents. In real life, as in reel life, Kate and Jo were ringleaders, mother hens to younger siblings. Jo had three sisters; Kate had two sisters and two surviving brothers. Family was the center of their lives. Forays to the outside world were adventures welcomed and encouraged, if only because they served as stimulating dinner conversation back at headquarters. About the only breach between the screen Jo March and the real Kate Hepburn was location. For Kate, real home—not the rental she kept then in Hollywood—was Connecticut. For the reel Jo March, home was the San Fernando Valley. Alcott's storybook tale of ninteenth-century siblings might have been set in snowy New England, but for Hollywood's purposes, Southern California's sunny suburb would have to do. Such practicality, Jo March herself might have admired. Certainly, the March clan, if not Alcott, would have appreciated the lengths to which the West Coastites went to make the sisters feel comfortable. RKO assembled the main interior set—the March home—with wallpaper, pictures, and furniture all based on real wallpaper, pictures, and furniture from Alcott's actual New England home. A pitch-perfect production from set to star. In the end, Kate called *Little Women* one of her favorite movies. It was real; it believed in the book, she said—just as audiences believed in her. Kate took on a popular literary heroine and found herself game. To read *Little Women* subsequent to Kate's performance was always to hear just a hint of Hepburn. She was Jo; Jo was Kate. A solid match.

Little Women was Hepburn's second film with George Cukor. Filming began in the summer of 1933. Just in time, as it were. Kate's costar Joan Bennett (*far right*), as flirty sister Amy March, was pregnant during the production. Quite an indelicate condition considering the movie's home-and-hearth theme. Suffice it to say, no tight-fitting gowns for her. As for the other usual near-calamities, there was the time Kate cried so hard and so long during a deathbed scene that she . . . well, vomited. Then there was the time Cukor ordered—*ordered*—Kate *not* to spill ice cream on her dress (only one of its kind on the set, apparently). Didn't help. Kate spilled ice cream on the dress. An enraged Cukor called her an amateur. An enraged Kate walked off the set. Then back to work the next day. As usual, one big happy family. With Jean Parker (*second from left*, as Beth) and Frances Dee (*far left*, as Meg) along for the portrait.

$\mathcal{K}$ate was alone. As in divorced. In 1934, she checked into a hotel in Mexico and registered as Mrs. Katharine Smith—a going-away present, as it were. She was there to see the Mayan ruins, and end a ruin of a marriage. There was little place for good-sport Luddy in Hollywood. While she played movie star on the West Coast, he remained in New York. On May 30, 1934, a Mexican court granted Kate a quickie divorce. Quite civil. Both agreed it was the thing to do. In 1942, they were divorced again. (Luddy, who would remarry, doubted the Mexican decree was legal.) On the court papers, he charged desertion. Kate, he said, "had decided that she couldn't continue her career and be married, too." That about nailed it. Luddy loved her; she loved—well, not him. Not that way. "I was a real pig," she would recall. "Always worried about me, me, me."

$\mathcal{T}$he curse of *The Lake* followed Kate back to Hollywood. To escape that disaster, she had had to drain her checking account and buy herself out of a national tour. (Why torture the good people of Pittsburgh, Chicago, etc.?) So back to Hollywood. But back to what? Her first film of 1934 was *Spitfire* (filmed just prior to the *Lake* debacle). Yankee Kate played a southern wild child named Trigger. "Her excellence in *Little Women* was matched only by the badness of *Spitfire*," the *New York Times* said. The film was not a success. Then came *The Little Minister* (opposite), a Scottish costume drama. Better, but also not a success. Under the direction of journeyman Richard Wallace (*standing next to camera*), Kate played Babbie, would-be gypsy and "daughter of a summer night, born where all the birds are free." That was how J. M. Barrie (*Peter Pan*) described the character in his novel. Kate gave a game try of it on film. Audiences were indifferent. Kate chalked up her second straight box-office disappointment.

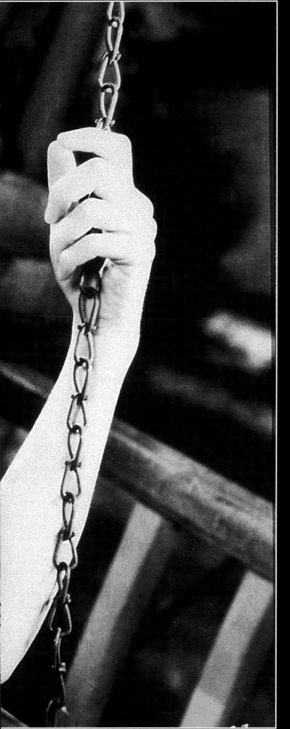

Alice Adams. No more Ozark Triggers or gypsy Babbies. Here, Kate was Americana Alice— determined to climb, climb, climb the social ladder—in this version of Booth Tarkington's 1921 Pulitzer Prize–winning novel. Released in 1935, the movie teamed Kate for the first time with George Stevens (*Giant, A Place in the Sun*). She liked Stevens. Obviously. They dated for a spell in the early 1940s, just before he directed her again in *Woman of the Year*. On *Alice*, Stevens inherited an actress—an Academy Award–certified thespian, no less—who had promise, he thought, but not necessarily the whole package. At this point in her career, he said, she had no technique. And didn't want any, either.

$\mathscr{A}$rrogance isn't a sin when you're a hit—and Kate was a hit. Again. *Alice Adams*, featuring stalwart Fred MacMurray (*opposite, at left*) as the no-status boy who manages to win her heart and Fred Stone (*above, at right*) as her poor but loving father, was a box-office hit. Enough of one, in fact, for Hollywood to forgive *Spitfire*. (As well as *Little Minister* and *Break of Hearts*—a 1935 romantic drama with Charles Boyer—both flops.) The industry bestowed upon Kate her second Oscar nomination for Best Actress. Come award night, she lost to Bette Davis for *Dangerous*. But no matter. She had stemmed the tide. And she'd done it by applying some muscle. She was now a star who got her pick of directors, and she picked Stevens. Is it arrogance if you're right?

𝒯s it comeuppance if you're wrong? Now *Sylvia Scarlett* (1935) wasn't "wrong," just an infamous commercial and (perceived) artistic failure. The bomb took out not just Kate but also first-time costar Cary Grant and good friend Cukor. "That picture had something gallant and foolhardy about it," Cukor said. To start: the premise. Kate is the daughter of a thief. In a bid to help him flee authorities in their French homeland, she cuts her hair, pretends to be a boy, and joins a song and dance troupe in England. The suit and tie (*above*) did not make the man. Kate, who as a youth regularly shaved her head and dubbed herself "Jimmy," pulled off being French about as convincingly as she pulled off being male. The funny thing was, independent Kate always liked to say she lived the life of a man. In *Sylvia Scarlett*, she did—just not very well.

After the first preview of *Sylvia Scarlett*, Kate (here with on-screen love interest Brian Aherne) thought the crowd was going to lynch her. Thought producer Pandro S. Berman was never going to forgive her, either. That last vision of disaster seemed certain. Berman, in a huff, *did* vow never to work with her or Cukor again. The pair's would-be "hilarious" comedy wasn't, not to the mainstream Depression-era audience, anyway. Cross-dressing? Androgyny? Gender confusion? Latter-day conventional wisdom said the film simply was ahead of its time. In today's world, what is a joke kiss between Kate, in drag, and costar Bunny Beatty? Film historian Vito Russo cited *Sylvia Scarlett* for introducing "the possibility of homosexual activity" in a film meant to serve both a "covert gay audience" and a "majority" audience. The failure, suddenly, was an iconic classic—although never to Kate. The film, she said decades later, "was a disaster and the reason why it's a success now is because the audience is a disaster."

$\mathcal{N}$o time for feeling sorry. Back in the saddle, as it were. Or back in front of the camera, as it was. In 1936's *Mary of Scotland* (*above*), Kate was again queen. She reigned as the so-called Queen of Scots, the sixteenth-century monarch. Mary was doomed, and so was the film. It wasn't a bomb of the magnitude of *Sylvia Scarlett,* but it was another Hepburn underperformer. As always, Kate put on a brave face. She had sensed the script wasn't up to snuff, but she tried to put it out her mind. What she couldn't gloss over was the fact that she had always chalked up Mary as a "bit of an ass." She said she would have much preferred a chance to play Queen Elizabeth. Now *that* was a role.

The original idea was for Cukor to direct Kate in *Mary of Scotland*. But, oh, that *Sylvia Scarlett*. Pandro S. Berman was *still* fuming. While he deigned to work with Kate again, he absolutely would *not* let Cukor work with Kate. It was best to keep those two troublemakers apart. So, enter John Ford. The Irishman had been a director for nearly twenty years when he took the *Mary of Scotland* assignment. He had made some fine films (*Arrowsmith*, *The Informer*), but had yet to enter his period of true greatness. Starting in 1939, Ford reeled off a string of classics—*Stagecoach*, *Young Mr. Lincoln*, and *The Grapes of Wrath*, among others. Unfortunately, that list didn't start with *Mary of Scotland*. Kate didn't think Ford had his heart in the project. He was a man's man making a royal costume drama. On film, Kate and Ford were a misfire. On the set, they fought. (Nothing new to a Hepburn production there.) But Kate liked Ford as a man. After filming, she took him to her family's summer home in Fenwick, Connecticut. Some sources say there was a brief affair. Others say there wasn't. In her memoir, Kate said they were "friends"—a friendship that she found "fascinating but impossible." She also credited him with saving her neck. On *Mary*, Kate insisted on doing her own stunts. (Again, nothing new.) It came time for her to ride a horse. So Kate got on a horse and rode—almost straight into a tree branch. Ford yelled at her to duck. She did. Saved her neck. Unfortunately, the film was not so lucky.

Mary of Scotland (featuring fellow Oscar winner Fredric March [*at left*] as the Earl of Bothwell) wouldn't have been so bad (and it had its defenders) if it hadn't been *Mary of Scotland*, preceded by *Sylvia Scarlett*, and followed by *A Woman Rebels* (1936) and *Quality Street* (1937). But it *had been*. Nothing seemed to work. Not John Ford's guidance on *Mary*. Not a tailor-made role as a women's rights crusader in *A Woman Rebels*. Not a reteaming with George Stevens on the romantic comedy *Quality Street*. With regard to the latter, the *New York Times* slammed Kate as a mess of "hand-wringings and mouth-quiverings . . . and eyebrow-raisings." Kate had had enough. In late 1936 she skipped out of Hollywood for the stage and a national tour of *Jane Eyre*. The reviews weren't as withering as those for *The Lake*. The production stopped in cities such as Chicago and Washington, D.C., but *not* New York. Kate's professional world was shrinking. She couldn't make a hit film in Hollywood; she couldn't act on the New York stage. Trouble.

Stage Door (1937) was a welcome respite. A great cast—including Lucille Ball, Eve Arden, Ann Miller, and Ginger Rogers (*at right*). A sharp script. A delectable story: Tart-tongued members of a showbiz-minded women's residential apartment strive for their big shot in the Big Apple. Audiences ate it up. There was just one problem: Kate wasn't necessarily the reason they were buying tickets. She was billed on the same card with *four* others. And she had had to jostle with Ginger Rogers—a much hotter actress at the time—just to land the first-line position. The lack of star treatment was jarring. It was a first for Kate since her ingenue days in *A Bill of Divorcement*. At least then Kate had had Cukor to protect her—and feature her. On *Stage Door*, she had Gregory La Cava. He wasn't interested in fighting for her, or even fighting with her, Kate said. She sensed she simply wasn't worth the trouble anymore.

$\mathcal{K}$ate tried a new strategy on *Stage Door* (*above*, with *Morning Glory* alum Adolphe Menjou; *opposite*, with Menjou and Rogers). Since no one much cared to discuss the finer points of the script, or the inner machinations of her character (rich girl Terry Randall), she shut up. But others didn't shut up. The future career prospects of the faltering Great Kate were batted around often—and in much the same fashion that the *Stage Door* girls dished (and zinged) one another at the Footlights Club. Director/playwright Garson Kanin (*Born Yesterday*) recalled overhearing such a girl-talk session on the RKO lot. The topic: "Kate—was she over?" The verdict: Mixed—until Lucille Ball piped up, that is. As dead-eyed as her *Stage Door* character, Ball told the group not to worry about Kate. She was a star, she argued—plain and simple. "She knows the combination to the safe," Ball said. "To everybody's safe."

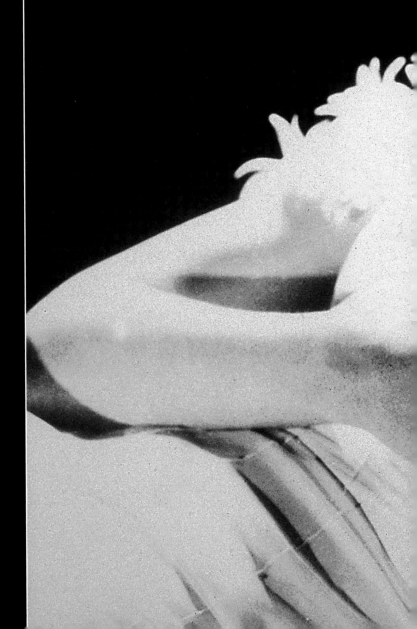

"*The* calla lilies are in bloom again. . . .The calla lilies are in bloom again. . . ." It was Kate's mantra on *Stage Door*. Her very own "Make my day" trademark for 1937, it kept celebrity impersonators in business for years. The line wasn't even in the script. It was just something Kate said so her character would have something to say during the film's show within the show. The "calla lilies" bit was a partially cribbed line from *The Lake*. Greg La Cava, see, didn't care particularly what Kate said. Told her to make it up. Kate didn't like to make things up. She liked to know exactly where she was headed. And after *Stage Door*, she did *not* know where she was headed. Or if she, like the calla lilies, would bloom again.

$\mathcal{R}$uth Gordon (*right*, in a 1937 stage production of *A Doll's House*) was an actress, a writer, and a friend. As an actress, she won an Oscar for *Rosemary's Baby* (1968). As a writer (with her husband, Garson Kanin), she penned the Tracy-Hepburn comedies *Adam's Rib* and *Pat and Mike*. As a friend, she was a forever one. Part of a foursome (with Kate, Spencer, and Kanin) that spanned some twenty-five years. Even longer, in some ways. Kate said she had had Ruth Gordon in mind when she was creating Eva Lovelace in *Morning Glory*. Gordon and Kanin married in 1942, the same year Kate and Spencer did *Woman of the Year*—a neat fit. The four-headed relationship had a complicated dynamic. Take Kanin's other good friends, for instance: Vivien Leigh and Laurence Olivier. Leigh was the woman who would be Scarlett O'Hara. So was Kate (sort of). Kate had read Margaret Mitchell's *Gone with the Wind* as far back as *Mary of Scotland*—and turned others on to reading it, too. She took credit for urging David O. Selznick to buy the movie rights. Word was that Kate badly wanted the Southern belle part. (Bette Davis was another big-name star who fancied herself Scarlett, among dozens, if not hundreds, of other hopefuls.) In 1938, it was announced (erroneously) that Kate was Mitchell's personal candidate for the role. Certainly, an event picture like *Gone with the Wind* would be a good bet to change Kate's fortunes. But Selznick wasn't sold. He saw Kate as a next-to-last, last resort. (He said he'd hire her before he'd hire Davis—both apparently equally unsuitable.) In the end, Kanin's friend Leigh got the part and Kate (herself a friend of Leigh) said she was relieved.

Is this the face of "box-office poison?" That was what Harry Brandt, president of the exhibitors' group, at the Independent Theatre Owners of America said. In 1938, he took out ads in the Hollywood trade papers, complaining that certain Hollywood stars were "poison" to ticket sales: Marlene Dietrich, poison; Joan Crawford, poison; Greta Garbo, poison; Fred Astaire, poison; Mae West, poison. Heading the list: Kate. Katharine Hepburn, queen of "box-office poison." How could that be? Wasn't she an Oscar-winner for *Morning Glory* (five years before)? Wasn't she an Oscar nominee for *Alice Adams* (three years before)? Nobody seemed to remember or care. Truth was, her flops outnumbered her hits almost three to one—and that was if you counted *Stage Door*, which wasn't exactly a "hit," and wasn't exactly "hers." Kate had good company on the hit list—one movie legend after another—but that was something to be appreciated with hindsight. Kate worked to win—not to be run out of town. But how to fix the problem? That was the tough one. To start with, what *was* the problem? The material? The image? (Not exactly a huggable one, thanks to her long-standing ornery relationship with the press.) Or was it—and this was the sticky thought—that she had not been very good to begin with? Success had come so quickly. Was it possible her faults had been glossed over, only to be exposed, bit by bit, movie after movie? If Kate knew "the combination," as Lucille Ball said, it was time to use it.

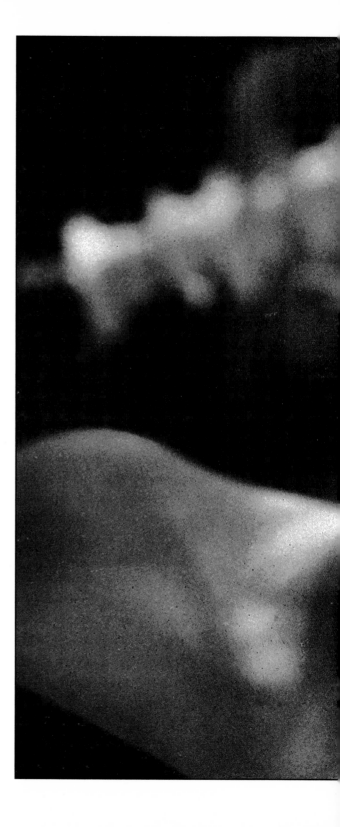

$\mathcal{P}$roduction on *Bringing Up Baby* began in 1937, months before the whole "poison" business spread. It was, like *Stage Door*, a return to the sort of thing Kate did quite well: playing herself, only more so. In keeping with Kate's signature parts to date, the Susan Vance of *Baby* is a mon-eyed, upper-class ditzy smart girl. The twist is, this high-society member isn't at all frosty. On *Baby*, the starched shirt was worn by Cary Grant (*above and opposite*), as befuddled scientist-type David Huxley. It was Grant's first film with Kate since *Sylvia Scarlett*. In an apparent attempt to avoid the failure of that effort, on *Baby*, it was Grant who did the cross-dressing. (Filled out a frilly bathrobe quite nicely.) The screwball plot concerned Susan pursuing David pursuing Baby, a leopard. Grant liked the film just fine—except the part about the leopard. First day on the set, the leopard, Nissa, snarled at him. He was a movement away from a possible mauling. Kate, on the other hand, got on well with the leopard. Maybe Nissa thought perfume smelled better on her. (Both Kate and Grant were regularly doused with toilet water—the odor made the cat more play-ful.) Nissa's trainer, Olga Celeste, said Kate would have made a very good trainer herself. Said Celeste: "She has control of her nerves and, best of all, no fear of animals."

There was so much right about *Bringing Up Baby*. There was Grant, in his comedic element. There was Kate in her element—right down to the golf course. And there was director/producer Howard Hawks (*opposite, far right*). Hawks was always in his element—whether it be a gangland drama (*Scarface*), a Western saga (*Red River*), classic Bogie (*To Have and Have Not*, *The Big Sleep*), or madcap comedy (*Ball of Fire*). Hawks did many, many things well, including *Bringing Up Baby*, hailed by the American Film Institute as one of the century's hundred best American films. (Only two other Kate films made the cut—*The Philadelphia Story* and *The African Queen*.) But if Kate figured this had to be the film that would break her losing streak, she was wrong. *Bringing Up Baby* opened in 1938 to surprisingly scathing critical notices and surprisingly paltry box office. The *New York Times*, in a state of seeming permanent annoyance where Kate was concerned, called her out for a role that required her to be "breathless, senseless, and terribly, terribly fatiguing . . . And we can be callous enough to hint," the paper's Frank S. Nugent zinged, "it is not entirely a matter of performance." Nugent's dislike of Hepburn in *Baby* bordered on the pathologic. The writer went at her again in a second column—deriding Kate as "a bundle of Forces, not altogether under control." Worse than that, he likened her to a "perpetual emotion machine." Nugent admitted that there was one Kate scene in *Baby* that truly impressed him—the one where Grant splits the rear of her evening gown, thereby providing "proof incontrovertible that Miss Hepburn has [legs]—and good ones." Now they thought her a machine? The snowball kept rolling downhill. Kate finally seemed to be paying for doing things her way: for appearing at press conferences in pants, for refusing to play the giggly glamour girl. The commercial failure of *Bringing Up Baby*, combined with the "box-office poison" ad campaign, put Kate at a terrible disadvantage with RKO. The studio sensed it was time for the kill—time to put its demanding, difficult leading lady in her place. It put Kate on notice with her next project: *Mother Carey's Chickens*, a B-film melodrama produced by the studio in 1938. It was doubtful that Kate, as a novice, would have come to Hollywood for *Mother Carey's Chickens*. It was unfathomable that Kate, as a thirty-year-old established star, would submit herself to a barnyard tale. And she didn't. Kate, always flush with walk-away money, bought out her RKO contract—and walked away. A six-figure gambit, but worth every penny.

The buyout of the RKO contract coincided with a Columbia loan-out. The studio let its falling star take a role in *Holiday* at its rival, provided Kate would turn over half her $150,000 salary to RKO. She did. *Holiday* (with, *left to right*, Edward Everett Horton, Binnie Barnes, Grant, Kate, and Lew Ayres) was a real homecoming. In 1928, she'd understudied the role of Linda Seton on Broadway. She'd even used a scene from *Holiday* for her RKO screen test. Cukor remembered. And though Columbia wanted Irene Dunne (*I Remember Mama*) for the movie, Cukor lobbied for Kate. The comedy reunited the front-line *Sylvia Scarlett* team—Kate, Grant, and Cukor. Grant was Johnny Case, the fiancé of a money-obsessed snob (Doris Nolan) who falls in love with the snob's sister (Kate). The movie was magic—and another troubling, inexplicable flop.

Fenwick. Back to Fenwick. Kate needed a change of scenery. Her family had a summer estate there, on Connecticut's Long Island Sound. Kate was reenergized by Fenwick. (Think Scarlett O'Hara and Tara.) She could play there, receive the counsel of her parents there, and act any way she damned well pleased without worrying about that studio executive here or that blasted reporter there. And so from Hollywood, in 1938, she fled to Fenwick. But the storm clouds followed. In September of the year, there was a hurricane. At first, Kate thought it was great fun—strong waves, whipping wind. Then it became clear the weather meant business. It really *was* a full-blown tropical cyclone. And it destroyed Fenwick. This was Kate's paradise—now it was battered and broken, like her film career. She vowed to rebuild Fenwick. She did. She vowed to rebuild her film career. She would.

*P*ortrait of a singular life—that was not at all singular. After Luddy, Kate never had a husband, but she was not without companions or lovers. She never had children, but she was not without children on whom to dote. There were nieces, nephews, the offspring of friends. There was her own flesh and blood, too. Kate felt more like a mother, to sisters Marion (*opposite, top left*) and Peg (*opposite, top right*). She was considerably older than they—had eleven years on Marion, thirteen on Peg. She used to say she expended her maternal instincts on the two. They weren't peers, as she and Tom had been. (The other brothers, Dick and Bob, had their own close partnership.) By the time the younger ones were in their teens, Kate was a star, able to help pay for their schooling (money became tight for the Hepburns in the 1930s) and their upbringing. But that was enough. "I was too selfish to be a mother," she said. Her father reportedly pushed her in that direction, arguing that she couldn't do well by a husband, a child, *and* a career. Kate said the decision was her own—one that she never regretted. The famous "No Regrets"—that was the motto. Kate admitted that, of course, she had *had* regrets. Doesn't everybody? The difference was, she never bemoaned them. No use in that. What's done is done. She couldn't fathom why she was later held up as a model of the protofeminine ideal. She, after all, hadn't done it all. Certainly, she'd done what she'd done very well—but she hadn't done it all. She *didn't* raise children. She *didn't* remarry. Those were choices—tough, adult choices. They weren't "for free," she pointed out. But if people still wanted to toast her for—what?—wearing pants, making a home on her own, and forging a screen career of sixty-plus years, then fine. "My style of personality became the style," Kate said. "I was sort of the New Woman at a very early point." The world had only to catch up.

$\mathcal{F}$resh-faced. Fresh start. In 1938, playwright Philip Barry (*Holiday*) went to Kate with an idea for a new comedy. There's this wealthy Philadelphia family, see, and they're going batty because a national news magazine is poking around—research on an upcoming article. Kate liked it. Barry wrote for her. Real-life Philadelphia socialite Helen Hope Montgomery Scott served as inspiration as the story shifted focus from the family to the family's eldest daughter, Tracy Lord—an icy socialite wooed by her ex-husband and finally defrosted by a journalist. *The Philadelphia Story*, Barry called his comedy. No one else but Kate was meant to play Tracy, and no one else did. *The Philadelphia Story* opened March 28, 1939, at the Shubert Theatre in New York. No avoiding the big city this time. "Box-office poison" played to packed houses. Kate was back. Hollywood was next.

The Philadelphia Story (right, Kate with costar John Howard) was hot property. And Kate owned it. Her beau, mogul Howard Hughes, had bought the movie rights for her prior to the stage debut. Any studio wanting to take the comedy to the screen had to go through Kate. Her first choice was Metro-Goldwyn-Mayer. MGM was Hollywood's gold standard—the glossiest productions, the biggest stars. The price tag was negotiable; the conditions of sale were not. One: Kate got to star. Two: Kate got to pick her director. Three: Kate got to pick her leading men.

$\mathcal{F}$or director, Kate got Cukor, recently and unceremoniously dumped midproduction from *Gone with the Wind*. For the role of Mike Connor, the reporter, Kate asked for Clark Gable. And for the role of C. K. Dexter Haven, the playboy ex-husband, Kate wanted Spencer Tracy. She'd never worked with either man. Had never even met Tracy. But she admired their work. Tracy's, especially. As an actor, Kate would say, Tracy was like a "baked potato." Complete, whole, real. Unfortunately, the baked potato was booked. Gable passed, too. MGM countered with Jimmy Stewart (*opposite*) and Cary Grant (*above*). Kate agreed. Stewart, best known then for *You Can't Take It with You* (1938), was offered his pick of

parts. He picked Mike Connor. That left Grant with Dexter (and top billing). MGM sealed the deal with a $250,000 check to Kate—$175,000 for the movie rights; $75,000 for her acting services. The Hollywood debut of the "new" Katharine Hepburn was set. "If the picture's a success, I'll probably revert to type," she warned reporters. Well, *that* was new, anyway—talking to reporters. But Kate knew herself pretty damn well—she was not about to be chastened; she was not about to be humbled. On the contrary, she had more power than ever. MGM got a whiff of the "new" Kate the day she presented a gift-wrapped dead skunk to a befuddled studio script clerk. She'd driven past it on the way to work. "I said to myself, 'I can use that.'"

$\mathcal{T}$riumphant—and in the company of the president. A sweet reversal of fortune. Upon its release in 1940, *The Philadelphia Story* was a hit. More than that—it was a record-breaking hit. "Box-office poison" gave way to Oscar nominations: for Kate, for Stewart, for Cukor, for Best Picture. (There were others, too.) Of the featured races, just Stewart won—earning what would be his lone competitive Academy Award. Kate lost to *Stage Door* rival Ginger Rogers for *Kitty Foyle*. But in place of the statue, Miss Hepburn had the newest, best-defining screen role of her career—Tracy Lord, the unattainable ideal who, through the right kiss, could be attained, after all. And as for the business with the president? Well, when you're a smash, everyone wants your picture. But it was more than that with Kate and Franklin D. Roosevelt. She was a staunch FDR booster. In 1940, Kate jumped out a single-prop plane and slogged up a riverbank to make it to a lunch at Hyde Park with the president (*above, at left*) and supporters, including son Elliott (*above, at center*). Nothing halfway. Nothing.

$\mathcal{E}$arly in her career, Kate was asked to name her favorite screen actress. Greta Garbo, she said—"Who can touch her?" Uncooperative Kate rarely gave a straight answer to reporters. (In one exchange, she claimed to have five children. "Three of them colored.") But her admiration for Garbo (*above*) was the real thing. The Stockholm-born beauty was imported to Hollywood (and MGM) in the mid-1920s. Mysterious and aloof, Garbo could create a buzz simply by speaking. (As she did, famously, in 1930's *Anna Christie*.)

$\mathcal{U}$sing the Garbo model, Kate created a sophisticated, womanly screen image. Both were best as inaccessible creatures—Garbo in exquisite, majestic costume drama (*Queen Christina*); Kate in high-toned society comedy (*The Philadelphia Story*). Never the girl-next-door types, these two. They guarded their offscreen (and, in a way, on-screen) privacy too fiercely for that. By the early 1940s, Garbo's reclusiveness manifested itself in her virtual disappearance from the screen. The student, meanwhile, was just getting her second wind.

$\mathcal{T}$he matter of how to follow up *The Philadelphia Story* was resolved easily enough. In 1941, friend Garson Kanin presented Kate with a story treatment cooked up by writer Ring Lardner, Jr., and Garson's brother Michael Kanin. Like *The Philadelphia Story*, it was another "for Kate's eyes only" project. The female lead, Tess Harding, was even named after Kate's real-life friend Laura Harding. The original title was *The Thing About Women*. It was a battle of the sexes comedy, circa the World War II era. In it, worldly, celebrated newspaper columnist Tess is pitted against streetwise, tough-guy sports reporter Sam Craig. The two meet, fight, marry, and fight some more. Kate saw the potential. She rang up MGM. Told them everything—except the names of the writers. (Michael Kanin and Lardner were unknowns—not exactly the first choices of a first-class studio like MGM.) The studio bit anyway, meeting Kate's demands of $211,000. Half for her, half for the novice screenwriters. *Woman of the Year*, as it was retitled, was a go.

Spencer Tracy (*at left*) wasn't sure he was right for Sam Craig. Or, more precisely, wasn't sure he was right for Kate's leading man. "We're so different," he told Garson Kanin. And even though Kate had wanted Spencer for *The Philadelphia Story*, she wasn't sure he was right for *Woman of the Year*. "We're so different," she told Kanin. The mutual confidant managed to convince each party that they'd work just fine together. Spencer finally agreed; so did Kate. They met to discuss the script. Kate, five seven and wearing her usual heels, eyed Spencer, five ten and needing not an inch of help. She declared him "rather short." Producer Joseph L. Mankiewicz told her not to worry. Spencer will "cut you down to his size," he cracked. That, the man did—Spencer thought Kate had dirty fingernails and deduced she was quite possibly a lesbian. Cue the violins. The most celebrated Hollywood love story of the century was born.

In 1941, when Kate and Spencer met, she was thirty-four and mostly unattached (the George Stevens fling aside); he was forty-one and very attached—in the legal sense, anyway. Spencer had married the former Louise Treadwell, a fellow actor he had met in 1923, during his theater days. He'd stayed married, too. Even in the face of a scandalizing romance with actress Loretta Young (*opposite*, in 1937's *Love Under Fire*). Spencer met Young at work—on the set of 1933's *Man's Castle*. It was an on- and off-screen romance. Spencer was mad for Young and made no secret about pursuing her, either. The press lit into them and it led to a real PR mess for RKO. Spencer didn't care. He left Louise and proposed to Young. She turned him down. And then she went public, issuing a statement that she and Spencer could never marry because they were both Catholics. (Louise, notably, was not.) Spence was spent. He never left himself open like that again—not even for Kate (*at left*, in *Woman of the Year*).

The title card on *Woman of the Year* read, Spencer Tracy first, Katharine Hepburn second. True, Spence was, with Clark Gable, Hollywood's most popular actor. And, true, Kate was recovering "box-office poison." Still, Garson Kanin asked his friend if giving Kate top billing wasn't the chivalrous thing to do. "This is a movie, chowderhead," Spence barked, "not a lifeboat." And so it was: Tracy and Hepburn. As an acting team, they would make nine films. The critics welcomed them: "Miss Hepburn and Mr. Tracy are all as crisp and cracking as a brand new $1,000 bill," the *New York Times* said of them in *Woman of the Year*. Audiences particularly liked the scene where Kate made a disaster of breakfast. It was a last-minute addition—one detested by Kate—designed to put her high-powered character in place. In the end, the film's would-be battle of the sexes wasn't really a fair fight. And neither was its stars' romance.

𝒦ate wondered if she was slipping. During the filming of *Woman of the Year*, she asked George Stevens if her performance was "too sweet." "Katie," her director said, "you get out there and be as sweet as you can be. You'll still be plenty nasty." A good line, but it overlooked the fact that "the machine" *was* different—and she was in love. Even the press—those old foes Kate used to be content to bash with her tennis racket—noticed a change. One 1943 newspaper profile declared Kate a "trifle" mellower and labeled her (with just a touch of irony) "Sweetness and Light." The reason behind the transformation was plain to anyone who worked on the *Woman of the Year* set. One day, Spencer and Kate were fire and ice. The next, they were in love.

*T*o the official world, Kate (in 1942's *Keeper of the Flame, opposite*) was still single. To just about everybody else, though, she and Spence were a couple. Her years of dodging reporters and their questions came in handy when it came to the affair. She worked hard to keep their relationship their business. Delighted in never giving the paparazzi an even break. Years later, she admitted it was the press that gave *them* a break—reporters looked the other way. Why? Maybe out of respect for them. Maybe out of respect for Mrs. Tracy, who, in 1942, founded the John Tracy Clinic, the renowned hearing-loss center for children. The facility was named after her and Spence's deaf son. John was the reason Spence never formally broke ties with Louise. Guilt and remorse. Remorse and guilt. Kate would not force the issue of marriage, would not broach the matter of divorce. She had what she wanted—Spencer.

$\mathcal{T}$he Tracy-Hepburn brand name was next attached to *Keeper of the Flame* (*opposite*). It was a timely, would-be noble drama about fascists (Kate's widow character was married to one). Tracy again was cast as a reporter—the crusading Steven O'Malley. The project was Spencer's first with George Cukor. (Kate was already on number six.) An actor's actor, Spence took to actor's director Cukor. Soon, he moved into a bungalow on Cukor's Hollywood estate. Kate helped try to make a home of it. That made one of them, because if it were up to Spence . . . well, he just didn't have much need, nor time, for "clutter"—from makeup to props to furniture to people. The early days of his relationship with Kate masked his larger problems, but not forever and not for long. Spencer was a lonely man who drank and suffered insomnia which made him drink even more. He was never at peace, Kate said. It was her mission to make him otherwise.

*T*here was no coasting for Kate. Not even when swept up in a consuming love. In 1942, she left Spence to go east and return to Broadway in *Without Love*. It was a new play by her *Philadelphia Story* savior, Philip Barry. Kate often might have copped to ego and self-centeredness, but she remembered friends—and she owed Barry. His comedy about a marriage of convenience didn't have the magic of his comedy about a divorce of means. But Kate still had the magic name, and she sold the play. It ended up doing well enough to go to Hollywood, where Kate starred in the 1945 film version with Spencer, reinstated as her leading man.

One of Spencer's most quoted homilies after his theory on acting ("Learn the lines and don't bump into the furniture") was his theory on politics—and why actors should stay the hell out of them: "Remember who shot Lincoln." Kate, the daughter of a "far left" mother and a "more conservative" father ("He'd have been considered a socialist," she said.), was not so easily dissuaded. She donated books to soldiers overseas, did a voice-over for a wartime documentary (1941's *Women in Defense*) and, later, stood up for Hollywood's labor unions during the messy studio strikes of the late 1940s. As the post-war Red scare heated up, the couple (*above,* at a 1945 Screen Actors Guild event) reportedly came under the ever-watchful eye of FBI director Herbert Hoover. His men dug up the dirt on their affair, but little else. In the end, Hoover decided against blowing the whistle on America's favorite box-office couple.

$\mathcal{I}$t was the mid-1940s and, unbeknownst to just about anyone outside her immediate family, Kate was nearly forty—the blasted middle ages. More like the Dark Ages for screen actresses. By 1946, Garbo was gone; Dietrich was past her sensation period; Bette Davis was in a pre–*All About Eve* lull; Joan Crawford had made *Mildred Pierce* and was on her way to *Johnny Guitar* (1954). Even Kate's *Undercurrent* (*above*) was neither here nor there—a cut-rate *Rebecca* about a woman who hastily weds a man (Robert Taylor) she later suspects of having murdered his first wife. But where earlier stumbles caused much teeth-gnashing, there was no such hysteria this time. Perhaps no more was expected of the Kate of "a certain age" (even if the world had no idea just how certain—or advanced—her age was). Or perhaps Kate simply had earned the right to a career—one that temporary failure could not erase, or heady success unduly inflate.

For all its shortcomings, *Undercurrent* was another first-class MGM production—in front of and behind the camera. The film marked Kate's first (and only) collaboration with director Vincente Minnelli (on the 1946 *Undercurrent* set, *standing third from left*). At the time, the future *An American in Paris* Oscar nominee was married to the studio's biggest, and most star-crossed star, Judy Garland. Kate got to know the couple a little. Not so much as to get engulfed in the Sturm and Drang of their lives, but enough to care. In 1950, when Garland was on the outs with the studio for whom she made *The Wizard of Oz* and at the end of her string with Minnelli, she slashed her throat in a headline-making suicide bid. Kate bounded into the hospital for a visit. "Get your ass up," she told Garland. That was the way.

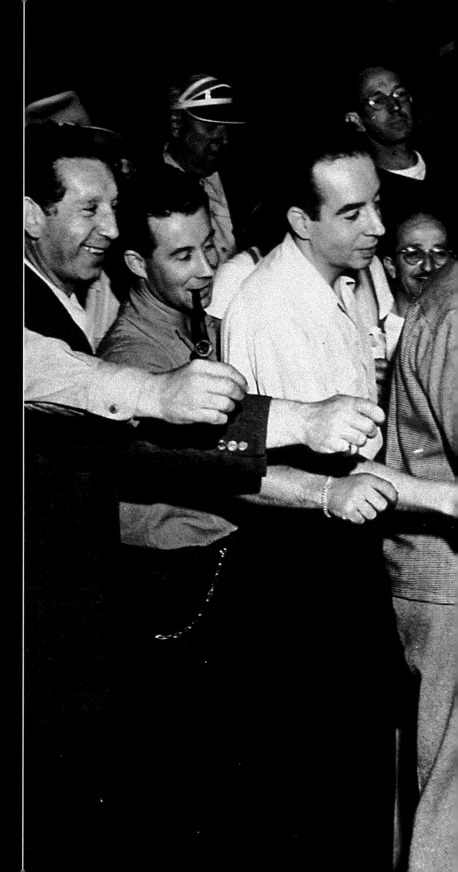

*S*ignature style by Kate—baggy slacks, tied-back hair, socks, sandals. "I know I dress like a freak," she said. But she didn't care. She dressed that way because . . . well, why not? She liked it; it was comfortable. So there. She managed her life in much the same manner. From her perspective in the mid-1940s, Spencer was likable; her relationship with him, comfortable. Perfect. No need for tinkering there. Careerwise, she sought out scripts they could do together—projects that would be both likable and comfortable. Searching for her own material became second nature to Kate. Though she never called the shots from a director's chair, Kate had been very much in charge of her professional self since exiting RKO nearly a decade earlier. For a while her job was easy: Find the new *Philadelphia Story*. (Indeed, MGM featured a clip of *The Philadelphia Story* in its coming-attraction trailer for *Woman of the Year*, lest anyone miss the obvious point.) But even just six years past her screen turn as Tracy Lord, Kate no longer passed for the fickle society girl. Her face was harder, leaner. She didn't look old—just older. Her acting had matured, too. The "hand-wringings and mouth-quiverings," while not entirely cured, had evened out. Her instrument, in a way, was purer than ever. But to put the instrument to use in a good movie—that was a task that never got easier. In 1946, for instance, MGM enlisted Kate for a project called *Song of Love*, a romantic biography of nineteenth-century composer Robert Schumann and his wife, the pianist Clara Schumann. Her leading man was Paul Henreid (*Casablanca*). During the production, Kate mastered the art of faking it at the keyboard (something that had troubled her so during the ill-fated run of *The Lake*). Well, at least, *that* was something. The picture, released in 1947, was not much of anything—slipping away with barely a trace. In the late 1940s at least, a Hepburn film without Tracy was not much of a film. The rugged individualist now was undeniably one-half of two.

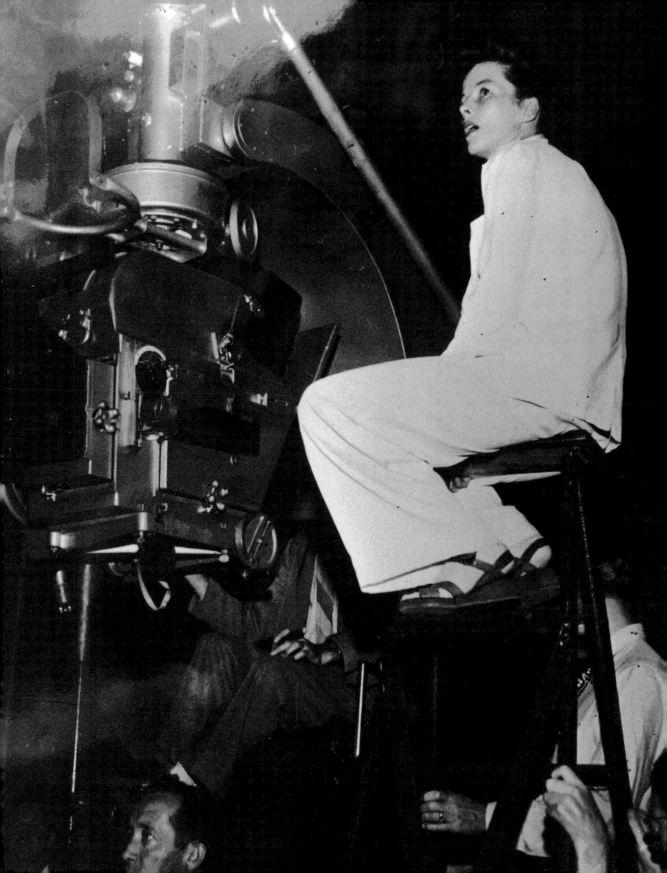

Though the press of the day restrained themselves from covering Tracy and Hepburn, they had a free-for-all covering Hughes and Hepburn. The leading eligible catches of their day, she was the young, mysterious, Oscar-winning movie star and he was the young, mysterious, moneymaking entrepreneur. Miss Katharine Hepburn had met Mr. Howard Hughes (*right*, in 1946, with actress Ava Gardner) on the set of *Sylvia Scarlett*. She'd heard he was interested in her. She'd heard right. And so began their affair. They were the odd couple who really weren't odd at all. Like Kate, Hughes was a moneyed, unconventional sort who did what he pleased. When he wanted to play at Hollywood, he financed (and directed) an epic (1930's *Hell's Angels*). When he tired of movies, he moved into aviation. Kate was one of his passing obsessions. They dated for two years. In 1938, newspapers breathlessly speculated that a wedding ceremony was near. Kate could have told them otherwise. She liked Hughes, but she didn't want to marry him. Once separated by geography (he on the West Coast; she at Fenwick, trying to make sense of her floundering film career), the coupling was **doomed**.

There was just something flat about Hepburn's middle period, the mid-1940s. Take *The Sea of Grass* (*opposite*), the fourth Tracy-Hepburn venture, and, arguably, their least memorable. Filmed in early 1946, MGM didn't release it until well into 1947. Some doubted the film would ever make it to theaters. Directed by then-newcomer Elia Kazan (*On the Waterfront*), *The Sea of Grass* starred Spencer—also looking noticeably older, if not outright old—as a New Mexican farmer and Kate as his unfaithful wife. Spence walked into the project after a trying spell. In 1945, he agreed to undertake his first stage role since heading to Hollywood. (He'd gone there for a contract with Fox some fifteen years earlier.) The play was *The Rugged Path*, by Pulitzer Prize winner Robert Sherwood (*The Best Years of Our Lives*). The title said it all—it was rugged all the way on this project. By then, Spence was used to film schedules that allowed him to lose himself in two-week alcohol benders. He kept his nose clean on *The Rugged Path*, but it was hard—not least because the play (directed by Garson Kanin) didn't work. At least Kate was there with him. She supported. She advised. And she scrubbed his dressing room floor.

$\mathcal{A}$dam's Rib (1949)—a sublime all-friends affair. Script by Garson Kanin and Ruth Gordon. Directed by George Cukor. Starring, of course, Spence and Kate. The promise of *Woman of the Year* finally was fulfilled in this comedy of a husband-and-wife legal team pitted against each other in a murder case. (He's the prosecutor, Adam Bonner; she's the defense attorney, Amanda Bonner.) Good reviews, good box office. This was how the world wanted its Tracy-Hepburn—bickering, battling, loving.

From Adam's Rib was sprung the too-brief film career of Judy Holliday (*at center*). Holliday was a friend of the Kanin/Gordon/Tracy/Hepburn contingent—a New York stage actress (a star in Kanin's signature play, *Born Yesterday*) who'd never gotten an even break in Hollywood. Kate and Kanin lobbied hard for Holliday to be cast in *Adam's Rib*. They wanted her for the role of Amanda's client Doris Attinger, a young woman accused in the death of her husband. Eventually, all sides, including a wary Holliday, agreed. Kate and Kanin figured the part—however small— could be her ticket to the star's dressing room for the planned movie version of *Born Yesterday*. Kate pitched in during the shoot, doing the key, single-take interrogation scene (all seven minutes of it) with her back to the camera—leaving all the lens to Holliday. Cukor called it the mark of a consummate professional. Holliday called it her calling card. She got *Born Yesterday* (1950—and with that a Best Actress Oscar.

Adam's Rib, Time magazine said, set the standard for sophisticated light comedy. But if there was something state-of-the-art about the on-screen relationship between Adam and Amanda, there was nothing so evolved about Kate and Spencer's offscreen love affair. Kate was brought up to "cater to a man," she said. His needs, his wants, his comforts—they came first. Always. That kind of sacrificial devotion wouldn't have fit the combative, cantankerous Tracy-Hepburn formula. But it served Spencer (especially Spencer) and Kate very well. "If you love someone, that is blind," Kate said. "That goes on forever. It's the magic of life."

*M*agic spells can be broken and blind love cured. As the 1950s arrived, Kate found herself in some straits. Whatever novelty there might have been in maturing—like the proverbial fine wine, as it were—was over. The bottle was cracked. As an actor, she told an interviewer in 1954, you sell yourself—the face, the hair, the entire pretty package. "As you get older," she said, "it becomes more humiliating because you've got less to sell." There it was—plain and simple. No, "Fabulous and forty" bunk for Kate. No, this was going to be a fight—a fight to keep the career, the body, the mind in order. To see Spencer all but give up his end of the battle—lose himself in the bottle again—was too much. After *Adam's Rib*, Kate and Spence hoped to find another "for-their-eyes-only" script. When none was to be found, Kate began to toy with the idea of returning to the stage—for the first time in eight years, and for the first time ever in a work by Shakespeare. Now *that* was a way to stay fresh. To goose the career, body, and mind into tip-top running condition. Spence, predictably, didn't take to the great wide open as, well, openly. Garson Kanin once said Kate lived in an expanding universe, and Spence in an ever-contracting one. Faced with the pleasure of infinite possibilities (or, as infinite as an MGM contract allowed), Spence chose to go on a binge. He was at a "most vulnerable age," Kate said—losing his leading-man swagger, losing his king-of-the-box-office status, steadily losing his health—and so he drank. This time, Kate asked him to do more than stop. She advised him to seek professional help. He didn't. Kate went back east to do her Shakespeare. There'd been professional separations before, of course, but this one felt chillier. It took frequent phone calls (from Spence to Kate) and new promises of sobriety from him to patch things up. But it was finished.

*Q*uite a rogue's gallery (at New York's chic Stork Club, circa the 1950s): ex-boyfriend Leland Hayward (*far right*); comic George Jessel (*second from right*); current boyfriend Spencer (*center*); Mrs. Leland Hayward (Slim Keith) (*third from left*); Mrs. Ernest Hemingway (Mary Welsh) (*second from left*); author Ernest Hemingway (*far left*). Oh, what this bunch could gossip about. Well, Kate probably didn't care. She was square with all of them. Especially Hayward. After all, he was the one who broke off their

fun—nearly four years of it—by getting married, in 1936, to actress Margaret Sulla-
van, which drove Kate to tears, even if she hadn't wanted to marry the man herself. It
was the principle of the thing. Anyway, Kate got over it. Two decades later, Leland
turned his charms on Spence, persuading him to star in the film version of Hemingway's
new novel, *The Old Man and the Sea*. This time, Hayward got what he wanted. The film
was made in 1958—one of Spence's best of the decade.

As You Like It (1950) was Kate's Shakespeare gambit—not to mention her best bid yet to impress her beloved mother. Kate had the notion that Mrs. Hepburn—dedicated social firebrand that she was—was not at all awed, or even cheered, by her number-one daughter's chosen vocation. Compared to suffrage and fighting against venereal disease, movies were frivolous things. But the Bard? Now *there* was some acting with weight. So, Kate gave it a shot. On the upside, she had no trouble packing houses anymore. Already she was regarded as something of a Silver Screen–era classic. On the not-so upside, the critics' notices were mixed. Kate as Rosalind, the play's cross-dressing heroine, was not judged to be the best match of actor and character—the star's real-life penchant for trousers aside. But perhaps the only review that mattered was that of Kate's mother. She attended and seemed to approve. Good enough.

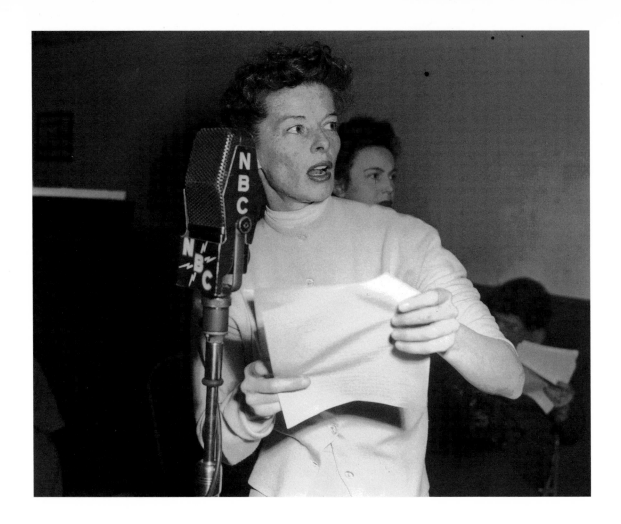

𝒦ate could be an affected actor. Kate could be a mannered actor. But, in the end, she was an *actor*. Whenever, wherever. Stage, film, radio (*opposite*, in a 1947 broadcast of *The Philadelphia Story* with Cary Grant), and, later, television. She moved freely among the mediums—a more European than American approach to the profession. The thing, to Kate (as to Shakespeare), was the play, the movie, the project. Kate gave credit too often to luck for the scripts that ended up on her reading table. But she really left very little to luck. A decade after *Stage Door*, in which she had played a green stage actress, Kate was still studying—under the tutelage of former costar Constance Collier. (In a real-life casting coup, Collier had played Kate's acting coach in *Stage Door*.) It would not be until 1994, after more than sixty-five years in the business (not counting any neighborhood performances she staged as a youth), that Hepburn finally suggested she might be ready to retire. "Haven't I worked enough?" she asked.

$\mathcal{B}$ogie and Bacall—the glamorous married alternative to Tracy and Hepburn. These two didn't bicker; they smoldered. Bogart was a leading man in the Spencer Tracy tradition—tough, no-nonsense, and no stranger to the bottle. Bacall, his wife since 1945, was a leading lady in the femme-fatale way—smoky-voiced, slinky, cat-eyed. Socially, the Bogarts ran with Hollywood's original Rat Pack. (Actually, they helped start the clique that later became identified with Frank Sinatra's.) That chummy circuit wasn't really Kate and Spence's speed; still, the two couples crossed paths. Spence and Bogie were old buddies, going all the way back to the 1930 prison melodrama *Up the River*. In 1951, an opportunity arose for Kate and Bogie to work together. A little adventure-drama about a woman named Rose, a man named Charlie, and a boat named *The African Queen*.

$\mathcal{K}$ate wasn't bowled over by the script. And she wasn't entirely sold on John Huston (*The Treasure of the Sierra Madre*) as the director. But she wanted to go to Africa. So she did. The excursion couldn't have come at a worse—or better—time. Kate's mother had died unexpectedly on St. Patrick's Day 1951. She and her father found her mother's body in the bedroom of the house in Hartford. Katharine Martha Hepburn was seventy-three. At least Kate soon had an entire continent to occupy her thoughts. Production on *The African Queen* began in Uganda and the Belgian Congo in April 1951, during the rainy season. Kate spent her downtime, hydrating herself with the local water and lecturing drinking buddies Bogie and Huston to do the same. Turned out that *they* remained perfectly healthy; *she* got terribly sick with dysentery. Kate could only surmise that the two bad men "had so lined their insides with alcohol that no bug could live in the atmosphere."

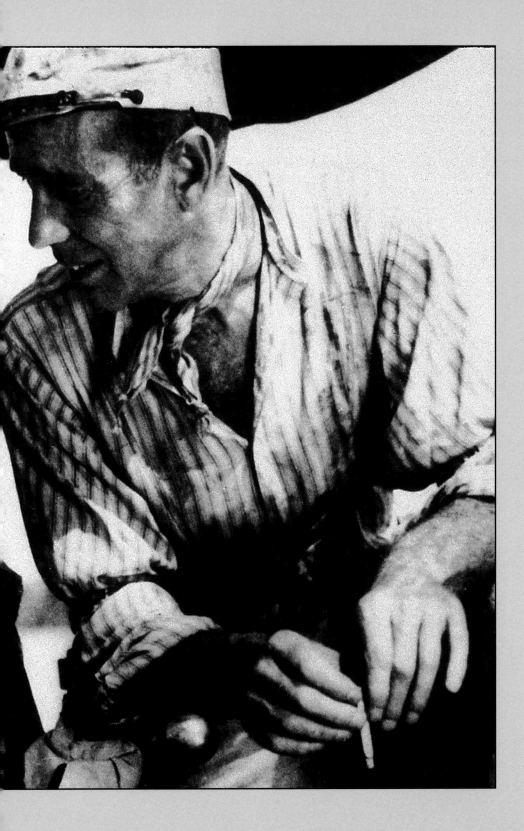

*K*ate's countenance tired Bogie. Here they were—miserable in the jungle, everyone complaining, except Kate. She found everything "divine." He griped, "Is this really the dame or is this something left over from *Woman of the Year?*" Overall, he found her all right, and she felt likewise. "There was no bunk about Bogie," she said. "He was a man." Their unlikely offscreen friendship translated into an unlikely (and tender) on-screen love. Kate's spinster Rosie and Bogie's rough-around-the-edges Charlie were a memorable Mutt-and-Jeff duo—battling the currents, the Germans, and the leeches. The movie earned four Oscar nominations, including ones for Bogie, Kate (her first since *Woman of the Year*), and Huston. Only Bogie won. Win or lose, Kate *felt* like a winner. She credited Huston with giving her "the finest piece of direction I think I've ever had." It was Huston who advised her to keep Rosie smiling. "Rosie does everything with a smile," Huston said, according to Kate. "Because Rosie *is* Mrs. Roosevelt."

I was a good golfer, a good diver, and a good athlete when I was a girl," Kate said. "I was so energetic." That she was. Kate (*opposite*, in *Pat and Mike*) didn't let up. She swam in subfreezing temperatures in Long Island Sound. She knocked around a tennis ball with whoever dared to pick up a racket. The athlete was as important to the Katharine Hepburn persona as the fine bones and the Bryn Mawr degree. It seemed impossible to avoid comparisons or connections with the actual person. Once, director George Stevens likened Kate to a baseball pitcher—a fastball pitcher: one who knows she's got a good, solid heater and keeps pouring it on and on and on—until, unfortunately, the batters catch on. That was where Kate was in the mid- to late 1930s, Stevens said. She was a pitcher in need of a new pitch. Kate, being the crafty veteran, got one— a curve that cut the corner off the plate. It was a pitch designed to keep the batter (and the audience) off balance. "Still got the speed," Stevens reminded. But she could mix it up, too. Kate often took guff from critics disappointed that she didn't loosen up and show more leg. (At least they sounded that way since they gushed enough when she *did*.) But Kate was no model of modesty. She had no problem "showing leg" in tennis whites or in swimming suits—as long as there was a point.

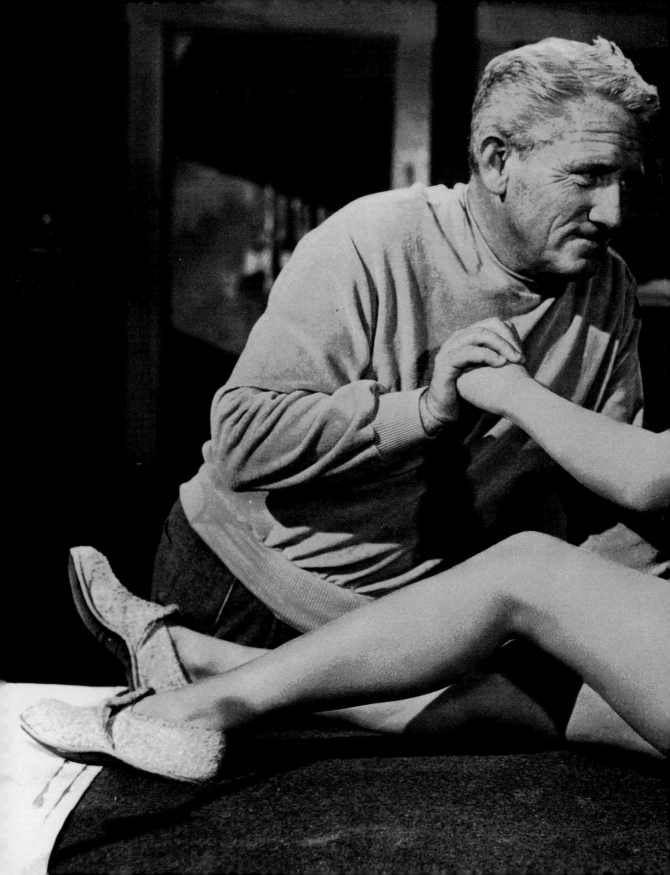

Pat and Mike (1952) marked a reunion of the *Adam's Rib* creative team. George Cukor was delighted. "I didn't mind accepting new ideas from Garson Kanin and Ruth Gordon or Kate or Spence. They were talented," the director said. "They weren't egotistical and always looking out for themselves. We worked together." This time, the Kanin-Gordon script found Kate and Spence in the world of professional sports. Appropriately, Kate was the athlete—the golf-and-tennis-and-everything-else whiz, Pat Pemberton. Spence was her shady promoter/manager, Mike Conovan. If you didn't know that Pat and Mike weren't cosmically meant for each other, then you didn't know the Tracy-Hepburn catalog. Their on-screen selves fought to make up. Worked nearly every time.

On *Pat and Mike*, Cukor sought to document a women's golf tournament faithfully. He fell in love with the footage, leisurely turning over the first quarter of the movie to the action on the links. He certainly had good stuff to showcase. In addition to three-time U.S. Women's Open champ Babe Didrikson Zaharias, among other pros, sinking putts on cue, he had Kate. "She plays a scorching game," *New York Times* critic Bosley Crowther wrote. "At least, it looks scorching in the movies—and that is all that counts." Have no doubt, Cukor needed no stunt swingers. Pat Pemberton's golf form was very much Kate's. Same with her form on the tennis court. In the movie, she squared off against the likes of Wimbledon champ Don Budge and Gussie Moran, a celebrated champ of the era. Summed up Crowther: "Miss Hepburn is no duffer."

While Kate was away, Spence, well . . . In 1955, Kate signed with London's prestigious Old Vic company to undertake a six-month tour of Australia with a trio of Shakespeare plays (*The Merchant of Venice*, *The Taming of the Shrew*, and *Measure for Measure*.) Even halfway around the globe, Kate heard the whispers: Spence was stepping out with starlet Grace Kelly (*above*). The future princess, ironically, would inherit Kate's role for the 1956 musical version of *The Philadelphia Story*, retitled *High Society*.) Kelly was Spence's first reputedly serious dalliance (outside of Kate) since Ingrid Bergman (*Casablanca*). Kate was book-smart, but she couldn't read Mr. Tracy. "Did he leave because he was bored," she wrote of an abrupt airport departure that Spencer had pulled years earlier, "or did he leave because he couldn't bear to say good-bye? The eternal question."

While Spence was cut loose by MGM in 1955 (a squabble over a proposed—and eventually filmed—Western called *Tribute to a Bad Man* ended his storied twenty-year tenure there), Kate parlayed her freelance status into another fine film, another fine adventure. The movie was *Summertime* (1955). The adventure was Venice. Director David Lean captured the city and his stars (*at right,* Kate, with leading man Rossano Brazzi) in a magical light. It was Lean's last "small" film before dedicating himself to epics (*The Bridge on the River Kwai, Lawrence of Arabia, Doctor Zhivago*). Not that the autumnal romance of a lonely American schoolteacher (Kate) and a worldly Italian lover (Brazzi) wasn't epic in its own way. Kate said Lean sought perfection in her, in every aspect of the production. The role earned Kate her sixth Best Actress Oscar nomination. There was a strong vibe for Italy at the Academy Awards that year, but, unfortunately, not for Kate. She lost to the Italian actress Anna Magnani for *The Rose Tattoo.*

*W*ater got Kate into trouble on the set of *The African Queen*. And it got her into trouble on the set of *Summertime*. Early in the film, her character, Jane Hudson, slips into a canal in Venice. The canals, though lovely to look at and romanticize, were not fit for swimming, drinking, or dunking. But Lean wanted the shot. The plan was to flood the immediate area where Kate (with costar Gaitano Andiero, *at right*) would be falling with canal-cleaning disinfectant. For good measure, Kate's exposed skin was to be coated with Vaseline—apparently the better to keep the nasty microbes away. All systems were go. Take one gave way to take two, then to take three and four. At the end of it, the canal did its number on Kate anyway, giving her an eye infection she never could shake.

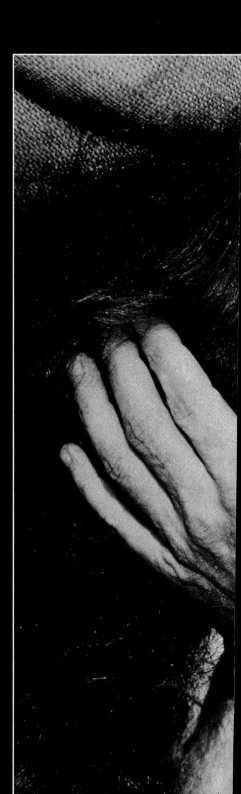

*A*nother year, another Oscar nomination. Too bad Kate didn't put much stock in the Hollywood award scene, because she was getting quite good at it. *The Rainmaker* (1956) secured Kate her third Best Actress nod of the decade—the seventh overall. (She wasn't getting any better at winning, though. She lost again. This time, to Ingrid Bergman for *Anastasia*.) Starring with Burt Lancaster (with Kate, *right*), she was Lizzie Curry, a vulnerable woman of, yes, a certain age. Lizzie finds herself swept up by a snake-oily Lancaster, in fine pre–*Elmer Gantry* fire. Kate came to the project a virtual perpetual-motion machine. (Well, she was always one of those, but . . .) She didn't slow down a whit from her far-flung Shakespeare tour. To the contrary, Kate immediately plunged into a sort of movie tour, reeling off three films in bang-bang fashion. After *The Rainmaker*, there was *The Iron Petticoat* (1956) a curious comedy indeed, pairing Kate with one-liner king Bob Hope. Bing Crosby, Kate wasn't. Spencer Tracy, Hope wasn't. In 1957, Kate held out for a film that reteamed her with the real thing: Spence. *Desk Set* placed the pair in the modern-day workplace, where computers (as big as houses) dominated. A lesser entry in the Tracy-Hepburn canon, *Desk Set* had its fans, however. As did *The Iron Petticoat*. By then, Kate (with or without Spence) had been around so long, she'd become the cinematic equivalent of comfort food.

$\mathcal{S}$uddenly, *Last Summer* (1959) was based on the gothic Tennessee Williams play. As was the way of Williams's work, the story focused on a southern family touched by madness. Kate starred (or costarred, really—she took a rare third billing, behind Elizabeth Taylor and Montgomery Clift, with Kate, *at right*) as the daft Mrs. Venable, a woman mourning a beloved son who died *suddenly, last summer*—eaten by young urchins. Skittish Hollywood tried to "clean it up" for the movie—confusing the point (if not the audience). Kate was not a fan of the script, reworked or no. Nor of the director, Joseph L. Mankiewicz. Reportedly, she didn't like the way she was treated; didn't like the way the troubled Clift was treated. (She was said to have spit in Mankiewicz's eye her last day on the set.) If Kate disliked the film, she had company in the critics. Her batty Mrs. Venable, after all, was the closest Kate had come to self-parody. The *New York Times* even gave her hair a bad review. ("Hepburn plays the matriarch and airy dowager with what looks like a stork's nest on her head.")

The reviewers could be downright prickly where Kate was concerned, cracking wise on the subject of her hair, her legs, her voice. The members of the motion picture academy, on the other hand, were absolutely hers. Even the disowned child that was *Suddenly, Last Summer* brought Kate another Best Actress nomination. (Her costar Elizabeth Taylor, here with Kate, also competed in the category.) That made four for Kate in the space of eight years. No one had a track record like that. No one. Only Spence came close. An Academy favorite himself, he also was back in the spotlight in 1958, up for *The Old Man and the Sea*. (Both Hepburn and Tracy lost.) The *Suddenly, Last Summer* experience was not a complete scratch. Tennessee Williams was quite taken with Kate, calling her a "playwright's dream actress." He went on to pen *The Night of the Iguana* expressly for her. Kate was touched, but she passed. The play wasn't her. And Kate was the absolute expert on Kate.

In the prime of her career, Kate made many—but not lots of—movies. By 1960, a contemporary such as Bette Davis had appeared in more than seventy films; Kate, thirty-three. While Kate never played ball with the studios (and their assembly-line system, which demanded heavy workloads of its stars), there was more to her relative lack of productivity than mere obstinacy. Quite simply, no other American star of her day worked more onstage. Kate was a fanatic about it— particularly in her forties and fifties. She didn't do just Broadway; she did Australia (with the 1955 Shakespeare tour); she did London (with George Bernard Shaw's *The Millionairess* in 1952); she did Connecticut (at the American Shakespeare Festival Theatre, in 1957). In 1960, she was back for more—starring as Viola in a production of *Twelfth Night* (*at far right*), and a month later, as Cleopatra in *Antony and Cleopatra*, both for the American Shakespeare Festival Theatre. A lot of work for someone who had started out just wanting to be famous.

147

*F*orget the reporter who remarked that Kate's "garb might have been snatched from a freshly laundered scarecrow." She could dress up when she wanted. Just as she could play nice when she wanted. "I think I'm very irritating to some people," she once told a writer. "It fascinates me, because I'm so sweet really." Then she smiled. Kate projected Kate on her own terms—*always* on her own terms. "I've done things for the honest reason that I like them," she said. "You can't do things just to be successful. You have to do things that affect you." In the early 1960s, she absolutely adhered to that philosophy. Except its application had nothing to do with work or career. The thing—the man—that deeply affected her was Spence. He was sick, terribly so. It wasn't enough to say the drinking, the insomnia, the profound melancholy had taken a toll. They were *always* taking a toll—bit by bit, day by day. Then, finally, they came to collect. Real, disabling ailments—chiefly, emphysema—began to plague him. In 1963, he was hospitalized following a breathing attack. It was all bad news from there. Spence needed help, and Kate was there. The days of crisscrossing the globe as a vagabond (if well-paid and legendary) stage performer were gone. The movies would have to wait, as well. In 1960 and 1961, Kate was a no-show on the big screen. The same from 1963 to 1966. In her absence, she worked to keep Spencer up there. He did four films in the early 1960s—two of which earned him Oscar nominations (1960's *Inherit the Wind* and 1961's *Judgment at Nuremberg*). Each project was an utter touch-and-go proposition. Spencer's health was as fragile as could be. Playing nurse, coach, and best friend, Kate got Spence through the paces. She sacrificed her career to help further his. Kate was the picture of the model wife that she never was to be.

In 1962, Kate suspended her self-imposed exile for *Long Day's Journey into Night* (*left and above*). (Spence had been offered a role, too, but declined.) The film was more than a screen adaptation of the famed Eugene O'Neill play—it was the play. Director Sidney Lumet (*Dog Day Afternoon*) did not tinker with the text. He even faded to black to indicate the end of acts. Kate starred in the harrowing character drama as Mary Tyrone, the well-medicated mother of a dysfunctional clan. Lumet likened her performance to "a mad courage." She even began her search for character in the furniture. Walking on the set the first day, Kate declared it marvelous and asked which of the living-room pieces were hers. "Each person always develops a fondness for her own chair," Kate told Lumet. The rocker was hers. So was another Best Actress nomination (and loss—to Anne Bancroft in *The Miracle Worker*).

153

$\mathcal{T}$racy and Hepburn. As inevitably as improbably, they were together again on a movie set. It had been—what?—ten years since they had last tangoed. Spence seemed about a hundred years older. The emphysema really laid into him now, coupled with some prostate trouble a few years back. But there was nothing like the medicine of a movie—a good movie—to rally the defenses. In late 1966, Stanley Kramer—the director who, as much as Kate, had coaxed and encouraged Spencer through *Inherit the Wind, Judgment at Nuremberg* and *It's a Mad Mad Mad Mad World* (1963)—had another idea for him. This time, the idea also included Kate. Smack-dab in the Age of Aquarius, Kramer envisioned a Tracy-Hepburn vehicle. *Guess Who's Coming to Dinner* was a modern social comedy, not a sharp-tongued *Woman of the Year* throwback, but still—the very notion flew in the face of the Summer of Love. Kate and Spence were up for it. The money people, knowing all about Spencer's health (or lack of), were more cautious. To get the deal done, Kramer and Kate put up their salaries as collateral—a show of good faith in case Spencer couldn't complete the picture.

Guess Who's Coming to Dinner featured the Draytons, a liberal, intellectual couple from San Francisco, who are suddenly forced to face their own unexpected prejudices when their daughter brings home a doctor—a black doctor—and introduces him as her fiancé. Established star Sidney Poitier (*In the Heat of the Night*) was cast as the intended, Dr. John Wade Prentice; newcomer Katharine Houghton (with Kate, *above* and *opposite*) played the Draytons' sunny daughter, Joey. Houghton was Kate's real-life niece—from the upswept hair to the fine Connecticut bone structure. *Guess Who's Coming to Dinner* was Houghton's very first film. Aunt Kate was there to drill, school, and tutor the twenty-two-year-old, as well as promote her—imploring a reporter visiting the set to "meet my niece." The Hepburn scion didn't go on to match her elder in film output or stature, disappearing from the screen for years after *Dinner*, but she went on to become a great friend of Kate's. No small accomplishment that.

$\mathcal{H}$e only worked mornings," Stanley Kramer said of his vulnerable leading man, "but he was a great worker." Sometimes the work was just in getting to work. The day before shooting was scheduled to begin, Spence collapsed—an emphysema attack. Production was hastily reshuffled. Tentatively, haltingly, Spence made it to the set—finding within him the power to deliver Matt Drayton's speechifying. His last on-camera moment found him granting Poitier and Houghton's characters his consent to marry—looking to Kate as he told them that if they shared "only half the love" he had had with his wife, they'd be more than all right. Kate's tears were real.

*P*roduction on *Guess Who's Coming to Dinner* ended on May 26, 1967. Spence skipped the wrap party. "He gets too sentimental at things like this," Kate said. Perhaps, but he also was sick. Nothing specific, just more of the same. In the early morning hours of June 10, Spence was his usual restless self; Kate was keeping her typical watch, sleeping at the foot of his bed, so as not to disturb him. She left the bedroom—only for a bit, it seemed. Then she heard a rustling in the kitchen, followed by an awful crash and thud. There, on the floor, she found him—as she'd found both Tom and her mother. He was dead. His heart gave as much as it could and then quit. Every time Spencer made a picture, Kate had said, he swore it'd be his last. This time, he'd been correct. The best Kate could do was hope he was at peace—free of the demons, the torment, the guilt. Of her lover and costar, Kate would remark, "He found acting easy and life difficult." Spencer Bonaventure Tracy was sixty-seven years old.

*H*epburn, without Tracy. Well, she hadn't managed that one in nearly thirty years. Since 1940, they were two—an old married couple, minus the paperwork. Of course, Spence was legally part of another old married couple. That left two widows—Kate, the covert one, and Louise, the official one. Kate telephoned Louise the morning of Spence's death. Told her what had happened and where. Louise sounded a note of mild surprise that her husband had died in the company of Kate. She thought their affair was "a rumor." Some rumor. In any case, Kate moved into action to ensure propriety to the rest of the world. She enlisted studio people and friends to get Spence's body out of the Cukor bungalow, free of prying photographers. It worked. No incriminating evidence, not ever. If you wanted a picture of Tracy and Hepburn, you had to buy a ticket to one of their movies. The same held true at the funeral. Kate didn't attend. She stayed away out of respect for Louise, out of respect for the children, and out of respect for herself. Kate chose to say good-bye her own way. The day of the services, she and her secretary, Phyllis Wilbourn, embarked on a covert mission to the funeral parlor. There, Kate helped lift the casket into the hearse. Later, she trailed the procession to the church—making sure Spence got off all right. And then she drove off. That was all she could do—nothing more. "Now you learn in life that the only person you can really correct and change, is yourself," Kate said. "You can't do that with anyone else." Not even Spencer. *Guess Who's Coming to Dinner* opened about five months after his death. It was quite a hit, with Oscar nominations for Kate and Spence. The night of the awards, Kate was half a world away—in France, on the set of *The Madwoman of Chaillot* (*opposite*, with a congratulatory kiss from director Bryan Forbes). She was awakened early—told she'd won. (Her first win, in fact, since *Morning Glory* a long thirty-four years ago.) Well, that was fine, but what Kate—who didn't give a fig about awards—really wanted to know was whether Spencer had won. No, he hadn't, she was told. (Rod Steiger took the trophy for *In the Heat of the Night*.) "Well, that's okay," Kate said. "I'm sure mine is for the two of us."

The Lion in Winter (1968) the title of James Goldman's play and subsequent screenplay referred to King Henry II. It seemed to work for Kate, too. To be sure, she had the regal air of a lion (or lioness). But was she really in her winter? That remained to be seen. Peter O'Toole (*second from left* in cast portrait) starred as Henry, the ruler faced with the gloomy Christmastime prospect of deciding which of his sons should be named successor. The cast included a future James Bond (Timothy Dalton, *far left*) and a future Best Actor Oscar winner (Anthony Hopkins, standing at center). And towering over all was Kate, as Henry's fierce wife, Eleanor of Aquitaine. "She's an ageless creature," director Anthony Harvey said. No, she wasn't in winter at all.

"I have this frightful habit; every time someone asks something of me," Kate once said, ". . . instantly, automatically, I say no." Unless it's a chance to star in a musical. The offer to do *Coco* (*right*) came in from lyricist Alan Jay Lerner (*My Fair Lady*) days after Spence's death. Lerner envisioned cinema's grande dame as fashion's grande dame, designer Coco Chanel. The composer was to be André Previn; the venue was to be (of course) Broadway. Even play-hard-to-get Kate couldn't resist. Imagine—her *singing*. Well, what Kate ended up doing wasn't "singing," but it was effective—and in time, too. *Coco* hit the boards during the 1969-1970 season. The show packed houses and picked up a Tony nomination for her. Friend Lauren Bacall, doing her own sort of warbling across the Great White Way in *Applause*, was up for the award, too. "Of course, I wanted to win," Bacall wrote, "but Katie . . ." Well, Bacall won. Kate was not crushed. The reward, as always, was the work—she sang!

*W*hen Kate was looking for movie scripts after Spence's death, location was very much on her mind. *The Lion in Winter* was good—that got her to England. *The Madwoman of Chaillot* (Kate as the Madwoman, *right*) promised France—even better. She would do the films back-to-back. Traipse from England to France—two countries that had the distinct advantage of being far from California and all-too fresh memories of Spencer. *Madwoman* was about a woman, yes, but not so much a mad one—more like an eccentric one. The film, on the other hand, was indeed a bit mad. The production was stuffed with bits and ideas and actors—oh, what actors: Paul Henreid (*Casablanca*), Yul Brynner (*The King and I*) and comic Danny Kaye, among them. But in the end, the film just wasn't there. Pundits said Kate, coming off the twin triumphs of *Guess Who's Coming to Dinner* and *The Lion in Winter*, had stumbled badly. Well, they'd said that before, hadn't they?

In 1969, some three decades after being labeled "box-office poison," Kate was named to Quigley Publications' annual list of the movies' top-ten stars. If living well was the best revenge, Kate was feasting. On Academy Award night in 1969, she earned her second consecutive Best Actress Oscar, for *The Lion in Winter*. Per usual, Kate didn't show to collect the reward herself. Too bad—she missed quite a function. For the first time in Oscar history, there was a tie in the acting categories. Both sixty-something Kate and twenty-something Barbra Streisand (*Funny Girl*) were named Best Actress. Freed from having to share the stage with the absent Great Kate, Streisand shone, holding court in a memorable see-through number. (Well, it *was* a pantsuit—Kate would have appreciated that touch.) Kate's win, by the way, put her career Oscar total at three—tops for an actress. It was a record that Bette Davis was said to have wanted desperately. Davis never got past two (for *Dangerous* and *Jezebel*)—even losing for *All About Eve*. Maybe Kate was lucky after all. "I don't think I've been punished by life," she used to say. Well, 1971 was a bit of a rough patch. Garson Kanin published *Tracy and Hepburn: An Intimate Memoir*. No one would ever believe she and Spence were just a rumor after that book. Kanin had outed them, delicately. There were no panting details of trysts and such, just a wealth of anecdotes about two good friends who happened to be a couple and who happened to be conducting a clandestine affair. Kate's friends—like George Cukor—were furious with Kanin. (Cukor joked he was upset because he wasn't mentioned enough in the text.) As for Kate herself? Oh, she certainly wasn't going to run her mouth in the press. She maintained a certain imperial imperviousness to it all. Claimed, in fact, never to have read the book—even as it climbed the best-seller list. One thing was for sure, her friendship with Kanin was never again the same.

*S*ince the commercial success of Oscar-winning *My Fair Lady* in 1964, George Cukor's career had slowed to a near-halt. Kate to the rescue. In the early 1970s, she agreed to star in *Travels with My Aunt* for Cukor. The script was based on Graham Greene's novel about an eccentric aunt who takes her nephew on a globe-trotting adventure. Wait—hadn't Kate just done the eccentric bit in *The Madwoman of Chaillot* and, before that, the daffy bit in *Long Day's Journey into Night* and, before that, the loopy bit in *Suddenly, Last Summer*? Hmm. "She would never admit it, but I know she didn't want to play another crazy old lady," screen-writer Jay Presson Allen said. Delays ensued. Kate didn't like the script. Tried writing it herself. More delays. Finally, she was fired. The studio claimed it gave her an offer it knew she'd refuse (show up for work in ten days, or else); Kate said she never refused. No matter. What was done was done. Kate told Cukor to go ahead anyway. He did. The film was released in 1972—with Maggie Smith in the leading role.

*K*ate on a TV set. Doing an interview, impossibly. Politely answering questions, improbably. Well, miracles *did* exist. The year: 1973. The place: ABC-TV Studios in New York City. The occasion: Kate going one-on-one (no studio audience allowed) with then-fashionable Q-and-A man Dick Cavett. "You want to sit back and look at her as you do at a beautiful rock formation or a splendid animal," Cavett wrote. The splendid animal overcame her suspicions of the medium to do the sit-down. After the two segments aired, she told Cavett she was amazed at the public's response. Stage, film, now TV—Kate mastered them all.

Kate had admired Tennessee Williams's *Glass Menagerie* for so long that when she first bounded into L. B. Mayer's office at MGM, imploring him to buy the film rights to the play, it was so she could play the lame ingenue, Laura Wingfield. (Additionally, Kate had envisioned Spencer as Laura's gentleman caller and Laurette Taylor as Laura's mother, Amanda Wingfield—a role that Taylor memorably created on Broadway.) MGM never did make *The Glass Menagerie* (rights disputes and such). And Kate never did get a chance to do Laura. But in 1973, she got her shot at Amanda (*right*). It was a tough assignment. Kate had idolized Laurette Taylor and her pitch-perfect portrayal of the emotionally fragile Amanda. And now to step into those shoes? Kate muddled through it, to mixed critical response. The finished product aired on ABC-TV on December 16, 1973.

*W*ell, this TV thing wasn't so bad after all. Kate was back in the small-screen way for 1975's *Love Among the Ruins*. The romantic drama reunited her with George Cukor and paired her for the first time with Laurence Olivier. Kate and Cukor went back to, well, forever—as did Kate and Olivier. Kate had been there, in fact, when Larry wed Vivien Leigh in a quickie ceremony in 1940. So many people that both Olivier and Kate had known and loved were gone. They really were the ruins, these two—cracked and crumbled a little, but still standing. And to see them standing *together*? That was a sight. Olivier didn't have quite the screen rep that Kate did, but his credentials as arguably the finest English-speaking actor of the century were secure. In *Love Among the Ruins*, Olivier played Kate's ex-lover, a fine gentleman who helps bail her out of an exceedingly embarrassing litigation matter. The telefilm aired on ABC-TV on March 6, 1975. Kate had mastered the medium this time out—sealing it with (what else?) an award. Her first Emmy. Olivier got one, too. So did Cukor. The ruins weren't so ruined after all.

$\mathcal{K}$ate didn't bother to pick up the Emmy in person, of course. Why threaten her spotless nonattendance record? About the closest she came to breaking the streak was 1974—April 2, Academy Awards night. This time, Kate wasn't nominated for anything—which made everything perfect. With no blasted thank-you speech to worry about, the coast was clear for her make it to the stage and present the Irving G. Thalberg Memorial Award to producer Lawrence Weingarten (*Adam's Rib*, *Pat and Mike*; with Kate). She greeted the black-tie audience in her patented pantsuit-and-clogs ensemble. Quite an entrance for her first-ever Oscars. Won her a standing ovation. "I am naturally deeply moved," Kate said. "I'm also very happy that I didn't hear anyone call out, 'It's about time.'"

Rooster Cogburn (1975) might not have been a big enough movie to serve the screen's quintessential hero and its quintessential leading lady, but it would have to do. Anything for the chance to see John Wayne meet Katharine Hepburn. The two legends were a mutual admiration society unto themselves. Kate likened leaning against Wayne's chest to "leaning against a great tree." For his part, the grizzled *Green Berets* vet found the kook from Connecticut rather adorable, actually. "Damn! *There's a woman!*" Wayne cried, sealing his last scene with Kate with a kiss. The movie was a sequel of sorts to Wayne's Oscar-winning *True Grit*. It found his Rooster Cogburn character trying to help Kate find her father's murderers. Most critics dismissed the film as a pale attempt to duplicate *The African Queen*, *True Grit*–style. The star power, though, was undeniable. By the century's close, a public-opinion poll named Wayne and Kate the greatest movie actors of the last one hundred years.

*H*epburn was nearly seventy now. She'd lived and loved and stumbled, but mostly succeeded. But what of the big question? The happiness thing. Was she happy? "I don't know what one means by 'happy,'" Kate once said. She liked to describe herself as being "happy spasmodically." She said "If I eat a chocolate turtle, I'm happy. When the box is empty, I'm unhappy. When I get another box, I'm happy again." And so on and so on. The age of the therapist's couch was not one Kate chose to recognize. She was a liberal, except where critical self-examination was concerned. Kate did not whine and she did not like those who whined. She did not blame her parents for perceived slights; she revered her parents. This was black; that was white—as simple as that. The no-looking-back blinders got her through Tom's death and Luddy's pain and her parents' subsequent deaths and Spence's death. Only with Spencer did she permit herself more than a little sentiment. The old Cukor house, for instance, was a virtual testament to sentiment. After Spence's death, Kate took over the rent, preserving the bungalow as an unofficial Spencer museum. His books, his clothes, his very toothbrush—left where they were, as if their owner were expected to return and reclaim them. Finally, in late 1978, Kate packed them up and cleared the house. It was time. She imparted some of the treasures—including a Hemingway-signed copy of *The Old Man and the Sea*—to Spence's daughter, Susie. The two women had become close in the years since Spence's passing. Kate liked that. Pop psychologists would argue that Kate was seeking closure; Kate would argue they were full of hooey. But whether she wanted it or not, that was what she achieved—closure.

$\mathcal{D}$own the road again with an old friend. In 1979, Kate and George Cukor (*walking together at left*) collaborated for the tenth time now on the television movie *The Corn Is Green.* "There's a complete absence of sham and nonsense between us," Cukor said. How could there be? He knew Kate when she was nothing but a "boa constrictor on a fast," looking for a job in the movies. *A Bill of Divorcement* was more than forty-five years ago—made when they were both young and wanted to show off. Now they were both old—and still wanted to show off. *The Corn Is Green*—first filmed in 1945, with Bette Davis—took them to Wales, where Kate played a spinster teacher who tutors coal miners. The movie debuted on January 29, 1979, on CBS-TV. After that, Cukor had just one more project left in him, 1981's *Rich and Famous.* He died on January 23, 1983, at age eighty-three. Another great friendship finally surrendered.

There was no way around it—the downside of being a long-timer like Kate or producer Hal B. Wallis (*at right,* on the set of *Rooster Cogburn*) was watching the not-so- long-timers pass on. So many greats— gone. Bogie, with whom they'd both worked magic (*The African Queen* for Kate, *Casablanca* for Wallis), departed in 1957. Spencer, of course, in 1967. John Ford in 1973. George Stevens in 1975. John Wayne in 1979. Then Cukor in 1983. Wallis even outlived Elvis (deceased 1977), with whom he'd hatched *Girls! Girls! Girls!* and other demiclassics. (Wallis died in 1986.) On Kate's personal roll call, there was Leland Hayward (gone, as of 1971), Howard Hughes (1976), Luddy (1979), drama coach Constance Collier (1955), and her father (1961). Kate herself didn't obsess over death. Didn't fear it, either. She didn't see the point. Just as she didn't see the point to wondering why people were born. "We're here after all, aren't we?"

$\mathcal{W}$it is out and crotch is in," Kate pronounced of the contemporary movie. That gibe aside, Kate wasn't the sort to sit around and complain about how things were better in the old days. But she did have a particular view—and in this view, the world had gone mad with showing things that were best left not being shown. Destroyed the mystery, as it were. So, what did all that mean? That Kate wouldn't be doing her own version of *Body Heat*? Fine—it would never have been right for her anyway. She found a good number of suitable projects to keep her busy. She'd done four features in the 1970s. There was *Rooster Cogburn*, of course, but also *The Trojan Women* (1971), based on the play by Euripides, and *Olly Olly Oxen Free* (1978), a confection about a junkyard dealer (Kate) and a hot-air balloon. None left a particularly big impression on the average moviegoer, and for the first time since her screen career began, Kate slipped through an entire decade without managing a single Oscar nomination. She was too far along and too much the legend to worry about what that meant. If anything, maybe it meant she was mortal after all. Clearly, the car accident proved she was not infallible. Oh, the car accident. That was in 1982. Kate was at the wheel, and faithful Phyllis Wilbourn was in the passenger seat. They were driving near Kate's Connecticut home. All was well right up until the point when Kate ran the car into a telephone poll. Phyllis ended up with an arm cast and a neck brace; Kate sustained a broken ankle. They were banged up but otherwise okay. Kate was a warrior. She'd had skin cancers (courtesy of her time in the sun on *The African Queen*), she'd had hip surgery, and she'd had rotator-cuff surgery. Bounced back from them all. The palsylike condition that became visible in the early 1970s, causing her head to quiver continually, was chronic but manageable. In short, she wasn't going anywhere anytime soon. Except to *On Golden Pond* (opposite).

On Golden Pond was Ernest Thompson's play about a curmudgeonly man coming to terms with his grown daughter and his own mortality. For the 1981 film version, Henry Fonda inhabited Norman Thayer, Jr., the curmudgeon. His real-life daughter, Jane, played his on-screen daughter, Chelsea. And cast—inevitably so—as Ethel, the clan's matriarch, was Kate. With Hank Fonda handling the workload as the crotchety member of the coupling, Kate was to offer one of her softest, most sentimental performances to date. Yes, she might just get the hang of this acting thing yet. Certainly, she was still working at it—even to the point of doing her own stunts. One scene, for instance, called for Ethel to jump from a boat and rescue a fallen Norman from the water. And who did the diving? Guess. Kate hadn't done such a feat in a good thirty years. But, well, why not? she figured. You can do one of everything, she said.

Between them, Kate and Hank Fonda had worked in film for a combined ninety-five years. And what luck—they finally had a project that brought them together. Kate was outright fond of Fonda. Called him a "little train," a man who chugged along on his own track—no curves, no detours, no excuses. She liked that. For the production, she bequeathed Hank one of Spence's old fishing hats. It seemed right. Norman Thayer, Jr., was a role Spencer could have handled, Kate thought. But that wasn't meant to be, was it? In any case, Hank was more than fine. *On Golden Pond* opened in theaters in December 1981 and was an unqualified box-office hit. Ten Academy Award nominations—including ones for Kate (her twelfth), Hank (just his third), and Jane Fonda (her sixth)—followed suit. Spring brought the awards ceremony and, in keeping with tradition, Kate won but didn't show. Hank won in abstentia, too. Unfortunately, illness—not stubbornness—was what kept Fonda away from the ceremony. Jane tearfully accepted on Dad's behalf and rushed the Oscar back to his home. Less than five months later, he was dead. Another one gone.

$\mathcal{K}$ate was most definitely not gone. In 1981, she was back onstage—back on Broadway—in *West Side Waltz* (*left*). The drama, by *On Golden Pond*'s Ernest Thompson, was about lovably crusty types on Manhattan's Upper West Side, of which Kate, as the piano-playing Margaret, was the most lovably crusty. The play was her first since 1976's *A Matter of Gravity*. No delicate flower, Kate opened the show on the road, then took it to Broadway, then took it on the road again. When she won her fourth Oscar in March 1982, Kate actually had the greatest excuse a seventy-four-year-old actress with a bum hip could have for not attending—she was needed onstage. Kate most definitely was still here.

The Ultimate Solution of Grace Quigley (*above*) was a project that had been kicked around for years. Something about the subject matter—an aged woman and a hit man join forces as mercy-kill missionaries, helping provide the "ultimate solution" to the elderly—made studio executives queasy, even in the days before Dr. Jack Kevorkian. Even Kate admitted her friends in the film business were "horrified" by the plot. Well, let them be "horrified"; Kate thought the whole thing rather witty. She also found it a cut above the rest of the scripts she was seeing—story lines, she said, that came straight from "the poor old thing department." To prove she was no "poor old thing," Kate teamed with Nick Nolte (*48HRS.*) to get *Grace Quigley* shot—finally—in 1983. (Anthony Harvey was on board again as director.) Despite Kate's affinity for the material, *Grace Quigley* was dumped into release in 1984—a forgotten misfire. Dispiriting, but not fatal. Kate was not finished yet.

For years, the sign in the driveway of Kate's Fenwick home made the wishes of its owner plain: PLEASE GO AWAY. But as Kate approached her eighties, she eased up on admission policies. Finally, she would share her thoughts and memories, in depth and very much in person. In 1986, there was the PBS documentary on Spence—*The Spencer Tracy Legacy: A Tribute by Katharine Hepburn.* Kate narrated; Spence's daughter, Susie, served as program adviser. The two even appeared together on camera for a conversation. In 1987, she turned author with *The Making of The African Queen,* an anecdotal memoir of her days in the jungle with Bogie, Bacall, and John Huston. Kate was hooked. Writing (and talking) about oneself wasn't so bad at all. And so, in 1991, there was a best-selling autobiography, *Me,* followed by its companion TV documentary, *Katharine Hepburn: All About Me* (1992). The recluse tag was still applied, it just didn't fit as snugly anymore.

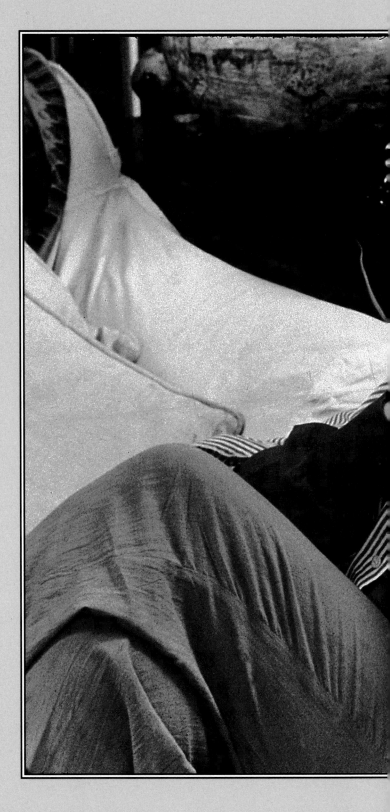

$\mathcal{K}$ate (*above* and *opposite*, in 1992) entered her tenth decade, working, as always. Careerwise, the one concession to age was that she seemed confined to working for television. Stage work was a bit much for the voice and film was a bit out of her realm (only so many parts for borderline nonagenarians to go around, you know). But television still called. There was the delightfully sappy *Laura Lansing Slept Here* (1988), *The Man Upstairs* (1992) with Ryan O' Neal, and *This Can't Be Love* (1994) with Anthony Quinn. "I know people say that she is scary to work with," Quinn said, "but to me, she is delightful." Fear not that Kate was losing her touch. In 1994, Warren Beatty lobbied, cajoled, and finally convinced her to film a cameo for his *An Affair to Remember* remake, *Love Affair*. She was back on the big screen—and she was back, period. Wrote critic Roger Ebert, "Hepburn's scenes steal, and almost stop, the show."

The Great Kate at eighty-five (*left*, at Columbia University in 1992). She had shrunk. ("I used to be five foot seven," she said. "Now I'm five foot five. I'm shrinking!") She was a little less robust. ("She's doing okay," a relative told Reuter News Service. "Her chief problem is loss of memory.") She was a little more private, even by her strict standards. ("She [has] retired for good from public life," columnist Liz Smith wrote.) After sixty years in the camera's eye and the world's imagination, it was time for her to go to Fenwick—and just be. Be in her garden among her flowers. Be with her family, her friends. "If you've been famous," Kate used to say, "you want to keep being famous." Except maybe not so much anymore. All things in their proper order. That was the way. "Would you like to go on living forever?" Kate once asked. "I say, 'No, please.'" All things in their proper order.

FILMOGRAPHY

KATHARINE HOUGHTON HEPBURN

FEATURES

A Bill of Divorcement (1932)

Christopher Strong (1933)

Morning Glory (1933)[+]

Little Women (1933)

Spitfire (1934)

The Little Minister (1934)

Break of Hearts (1935)

Alice Adams (1935)*

Sylvia Scarlett (1935)

Mary of Scotland (1936)

A Woman Rebels (1936)

Quality Street (1937)

Stage Door (1937)

Bringing Up Baby (1938)

Holiday (1938)

The Philadelphia Story (1940)*

Woman of the Year (1942)*

Keeper of the Flame (1942)

Stage Door Canteen (1943)

Dragon Seed (1944)

Without Love (1945)

Undercurrent (1946)

The Sea of Grass (1947)

Song of Love (1947)

State of the Union (1948)

Adam's Rib (1949)

The African Queen (1951)*

Pat and Mike (1952)

Summertime (1955)*

The Rainmaker (1956)*

The Iron Petticoat (1956)

Desk Set (1957)

Suddenly, Last Summer (1959)*

Long Day's Journey into Night (1962)*

Guess Who's Coming to Dinner (1967)[+]

The Lion in Winter (1968)[+]

The Madwoman of Chaillot (1969)

The Trojan Women (1971)

A Delicate Balance (1973)

Rooster Cogburn (1975)

Olly Olly Oxen Free (1978)

On Golden Pond (1981)[+]

The Ultimate Solution of Grace Quigley
    (*aka* Grace Quigley) (1984)

Love Affair (1994)

* Academy Award nomination—Best Actress
[+] Academy Award winner—Best Actress

TELEVISION

The Glass Menagerie (1973)*

Love Among the Ruins (1975)+

The Corn Is Green (1979)*

The Spencer Tracy Legacy: A Tribute by Katharine
    Hepburn (1986)

Mrs. Delafield Wants to Marry (1986)*

Laura Lansing Slept Here (1988)

Katharine Hepburn: All About Me (1992)**

The Man Upstairs (1992)

This Can't Be Love (1994)

One Christmas (1994)

* Emmy nomination—Outstanding Lead Actress
    (Miniseries or Special)
[+] Emmy win—Outstanding Actress (Miniseries or
    Special)
** Emmy nomination—Outstanding
    Informational Special

BIBLIOGRAPHY

BOOKS

Anderson, Christopher. *An Affair to Remember: The Remarkable Love Story of Katharine Hepburn and Spencer Tracy*. New York: William Morrow, 1997.

Bacall, Lauren. *By Myself*. New York: Alfred A. Knopf, 1978.

Billingsley, Kenneth Lloyd. *Hollywood Party*. New York: Forum/Prism, 1998.

Edwards, Anne. *A Remarkable Woman: A Biography of Katharine Hepburn*. New York: William Morrow, 1985.

Farnighetti, Robert (editor). *The World Almanac and Book of Facts*. New York: Funk & Wagnalls, 1994.

Frank, Gerold. *Judy*. New York: Harper & Row, 1975.

Hepburn, Katharine. *The Making of "The African Queen": Or How I Went to Africa with Bogart, Bacall and Houston and Almost Lost My Mind*. New York: Alfred A. Knopf, 1987.

Hepburn, Katharine. *Me: Stories of My Life*. New York: Random House, 1991.

Kanin, Garson. *Tracy and Hepburn: An Intimate Memoir*. New York: Viking Press, 1971.

Leverich, Lyle. *Tom: The Unknown Tennessee Williams*. New York: Crown, 1995.

Lumet, Sidney. *Making Movies*. New York: Alfred A. Knopf, 1995.

Macpherson, Don, and Louise Brody. *Leading Ladies*. New York: St. Martin's Press, 1986.

Maltin, Leonard (editor). *Leonard Maltin's 1997 Movie & Video Guide*. New York: Signet, 1996.

McGilligan, Patrick. *George Cukor: A Double Life*. New York: St. Martin's Press, 1991.

McNeil, Alex. *Total Television*. New York: Penguin Books, 1996.

Roberts, Randy, and James S. Olsen. *John Wayne: American*. Colorado: Bison Books, 1997.

Russo, Vito. *The Celluloid Closet*. New York: Harper & Row, 1987.

Sarris, Andrew. *The American Cinema: Directors and Directions, 1928–1968*. New York: Da Capo Press, 1996.

Scheuer, Steven H. (editor). *Movies on TV and Videocassette 1991–92*. New York: Bantam Books, 1990.

INTERNET

Baseline (*www.pkbaseline.com*) (biographies—Katharine Hepburn, Spencer Tracy)

E! Online (*www.eonline.com*) ("Gwyneth Who?"—Katharine Hepburn named century's greatest screen actress)

John Tracy Clinic (*www.johntracyclinic.org*) (background/ history of clinic)

Internet Movie Database (*www.imdb.com*) (general filmographies)

RESEARCH ASSISTANCE

Stuart Galbraith IV
John T. Ryan